The History of Racism:

A Guide to White Supremacy

Corey White

Library of Congress Control Number: 2026903057
Paperback ISBN: 979-8-9947817-0-8
Book formatted: Arilia Winn, Winn Publications

The History of Racism:

A Guide to White Supremacy

TABLE OF CONTENTS

Preface   vii

Chapter 1. 1492: The Doctrine of Discovery   1
Chapter 2. 1619: The Casual Killing Act   9
Chapter 3. The Door of No Return: Signs of Insurrections   19
Chapter 4. American Revolution: The Illusion of Whiteness   31
Chapter 5. The American Constitution: Broken Promises   41
Chapter 6. The Fugitive Acts: A Revolution in Haiti   51
Chapter 7. The Caste System: A Struggle for Power   61
Chapter 8. 1804: The 2nd War for Independence   71
Chapter 9. Searching for Freedom: The First Seminole War   81
Chapter 10. Denmark's Rebellion: The Second Middle Passage   91
Chapter 11. Jump Jim Crow: Nat Turner's Revolt   101
Chapter 12. The Second Seminole War: A Trail of Tears   111
Chapter 13 Manifest Destiny: The Dred Scott Decision   121
Chapter 14. Fugitive Slave Acts: The Great Escape   131
Chapter 15. Declaration of a Civil War: The Homestead Act   141
Chapter 16. An Emancipation Proclamation: The Draft Riots   151
Chapter 17 Juneteenth: 40 Acres and a Mule   161

Epilogue.   171
Acknowledgments   173

PREFACE

First, I want to thank the ancestors for the opportunity and inspiration to create this book. Please allow me to do the ancestors, myself, and the audience justice, as well as all those who have faced injustice. This book is not about the history of the world or the history of Black people, as that history goes far beyond racism. This book is not about the history of slavery, religious persecution, or other inhumane systems of oppression such as the Arab slave trade, although those topics must be addressed as well. This book is not about who we are as a people, where we come from, what we should call ourselves, or what we did before the system of white supremacy. It isn't even about any event or person mentioned in the book. I encourage you to do your own research on the details that aren't in this book and on the information that is. This text is about the history of white supremacy, how it developed, how it still affects us, and, most importantly, how to fight it. This system wasn't created overnight. It was cultivated over centuries. So much Black history has been destroyed or lost. It is important we learn as much of our history as possible. This is not only to prevent history from repeating, but to discover what we're capable of moving forward. Together, we'll re-experience everything, from the lowest of the lows to the highest of the highs, from a Black perspective on this journey of colonization. Thank you to everyone who made this possible.

As a man thinketh, so is he!

CHAPTER 1.
1492: THE DOCTRINE OF DISCOVERY

As Christopher Columbus laid eyes on the "new world" for the first time, little did he know he'd get credit and his own holiday for ushering in a new era of colonialism. The concept of racism itself hasn't always existed. And when we understand how it originated and gained traction, we can begin to fight back. Our story does not start in 1492, however. By then, decades of systematic kidnapping and land grabbing had already begun.

Years before Columbus was born, the Portuguese established a trading outpost on the island of Arguin, near Mauritania in 1445, as myths of the African savage spread. Of course, the Spanish and Portuguese used these myths to justify their savage crimes of kidnapping, rape, and murder. But first, we need to understand what "savage" means to Europeans. Typically, when they've come across a group or person who doesn't know or refuses to follow European culture or laws, or bow down to European deities, they label them savages who must be shown the way to salvation.

You must be Europeanized to be civilized. In reality, conquering the land, taking the resources, and enslaving the people was the goal. But to sleep at night, they told themselves the people weren't human, only savages.

In 1441, Portuguese sailors took the first kidnapped West Africans back to Europe. In 1444, 235 more were captured, effectively beginning the slave trade. By the end of June 1452, Pope Nicholas V issued a papal bull called the Dum Diversas. It granted Spain and Portugal full permission to search out, invade, capture, and subjugate non-believers of Christ. The goal of the Catholic church was to reduce non-Christians, or pagans, into perpetual servitude while taking their land. Nicholas V issued a follow up papal bull in 1455. The Romanus Pontifex extended Catholic nations of European dominion over "discovered" land.

When Columbus entered the picture, Portuguese and Spanish roots were already established. Funded by Spain and aided by the Niño brothers and other melanated crew members, Columbus landed in the Caribbean region in 1492. They never made it to North America or India, despite calling the natives Indians. After Columbus found gold and other natural resources, greed took over. He destroyed and pillaged his way through Hispaniola.

More important than gold, Columbus saw the value of the native people as laborers. He saw how welcoming and naive they were, yet unable to protect themselves. Columbus took gold and other resources, including people, back to Spain. He wanted to show how easy they were to enslave and to send more troops to take the land. In addition to guns, Europeans brought diseases, making it easier for them to capture natives. Still, Columbus felt he wasn't getting as much gold as he wanted.

Columbus made his second trip in 1493, despite doubts about the legality of slave trading. Several hundred people were shipped from Hispaniola to Spain. Countless more were captured, and Columbus forced them to mine gold. When anyone resisted, he cut off their hands, feet, ears, tongue, or simply beheaded them. Women and little girls were viciously raped; if they resisted, they were beaten into submission. Babies were taken out of their mother's arms and fed to attack dogs. Entire villages were burned.

Even Columbus's peers condemned his actions, saying they'd never seen anything so savage. When Spanish rulers learned of Columbus's crimes, he was stripped of his title as governor, arrested, and shipped back to Spain. Although Columbus once called the natives peaceful and nice, to justify his crimes, he said, "They are evil; they eat men. They're savage cannibals with dog-like noses that drink their victim's blood." Many Spaniards, including the king, opposed Columbus being arrested. King Ferdinand freed Columbus, restored his wealth, and agreed to fund one last voyage.

Pope Alexander VI also sided with Columbus, issuing another papal bull in 1493. The Inter Caetera gave Spain and Portugal the rights to lands west and south of Cape Verde. However, one Christian nation had no right to conquer land already conquered by another Christian nation.

Incidentally, the illegitimate son of Alexander VI was Cesare Borgia. Some say the image of Jesus we've seen growing up in Black churches and homes is actually Borgia.

The Portuguese and Spanish were in a race to conquer land and enslave people. Genocides on the native population were so frequent, they nearly went extinct. Europeans agreed trafficking Africans was the best way to replace the slave population. Ferdinand II allowed enslaved Africans to be brought into Spanish colonies for the first time in 1501. His only condition was they already be Christianized. Jews, Moors, and newly converted Christians were forbidden. While countless people were kidnapped, the King of Kongo was baptized by Portuguese officials. Afonso I became the first Catholic king in Kongo in 1506.

One of the earliest recorded slave shipments arrived in the "new world" in 1502. Juan de Córdoba was the first merchant identified who was authorized by the Spanish to send slaves, although it was in minuscule numbers. By the time the first kidnapped Africans reached Hispaniola in 1511, Ponce De León was sent looking for more gold. He landed in Florida, which included the Carolinas, and claimed the land for Spain by 1513. De León and his crew encountered hostility from an unwelcoming native tribe and were forced back to their ships.

Although there were many tribes in Florida, the Calusa tribe was the only tribe that was identified. When De León returned in 1521, they attacked again, mortally wounding him.

Everyone didn't just go quietly. Many people fought for their lives. The majority of history is left out of most books, but people have been fighting colonialism since day one. The revolt of Enriquillo was one of the earliest recorded rebellions between 1519-1533. Enriquillo (Enrique) created an army of rebels armed with whatever weapons they could find, be it a rock, stick, or a spear they made. Enriquillo told them to only fight in self-defense, only kill in battle, and, if possible, to just try to disarm them. They were successful enough to force the Spanish to offer a peace treaty, but the damage was already done. Weapons and diseases took its toll on the people, not to mention suicides in mass numbers. Women killed their children and aborted babies to avoid a life of slavery because to them, death was better than bondage.

Some believe Wolof African slaves taught the Taino rebels how to organize and defend themselves against the Spanish. They also led the Santo Domingo Slave Revolt of 1521, or the Great Wolof Scare. Although its unclear if it took place around Christmas 1521 or January 1522, it was the first time African slaves joined with the indigenous population to fight enslavement.

According to oral traditions, the revolt was led by a Wolof couple, Maria Olofa and Gonzalo Mandinga on a Nueva Isabela plantation owned by Diego Colon, the son of Christopher Columbus.

Although they were seeking freedom, according to the Spanish, their goal was to kill all Christians and take over the land. They attacked farms and plantations, taking resources, weapons, and freeing other slaves, many of whom joined them. After a few days, the rebellion was put down by a militia led by Colon. The alleged leaders of the rebellion was executed and the others were harshly punished. By January 6, 1522, Colon introduced the first race-based laws in the "new world." Both free and enslaved Africans access to weapons was minimized and they were restricted from moving around freely . Anyone found guilty of leading a rebellion was to be put to death, while everyone else was to be tortured.

Numerous revolts exploded throughout the "new world," including the 1522 slave revolt in Hispaniola. On Christmas day, twenty African Muslims attacked their enslavers. They killed several Spaniards and freed dozens of people. There were several more attempts to end colonization throughout the 1530s.

Despite resistance, the slave trade escalated significantly. King Charles I of Spain granted the first licenses to transport Africans to the "new world" in 1518. More than 4,000 people were imported, and thousands more were sent each year after that. As more Europeans arrived in the Americas, the violence intensified and the race for the "new world" persisted. By 1521, Hernán Cortés had already destroyed the Aztec empire, and the Inca empire was gone by 1533.

Spanish colonizers landed in what became Georgia and South Carolina in 1526. They brought 100 enslaved Africans with them, possibly the first enslaved Africans taken to North America. With the help of nearby natives, the enslaved Africans set fire to the colony and escaped by blending in with native tribes in what was known as the San Miguel De Gualdape Rebellion.

The African population in Hispaniola grew to over 30,000 by 1542. With the native population decimated, the Spanish decided to abolish Indian slavery in their colonies. The next year, a Spanish decree prohibited enslaving Muslims who were converted to Christianity. But in 1550, the Portuguese sent the first slaves to Brazil, who were kidnapped directly from Africa.

Upon their arrival, uprisings spread throughout the Caribbean like wildfire. Between 1550-1552, the first insurrections in Nicaragua, Peru, Venezuela, as well as the Bayano Wars in Panama, took place. King Bayano and his army were able to defeat the Spanish. They freed themselves and established their own community with natives in the area. During his reign, King Bayano attacked several Spanish slave markets and freed as many people as possible. He forced the Spanish governor to offer a treaty, but it was only a trap. When Bayano and his men met with the Spanish to sign the treaty unarmed, they were poisoned.

Africans outnumbered Europeans 15 to 1 in Hispaniola by 1560. The first major example on record of England participating in the slave trade wasn't until 1562. English sailors transported 300 Africans from Sierra Leone to Hispaniola. They illegally traded with the Spanish, contributing to growing tensions between England and Spain. As England got a taste of the slave trade, the Spanish continued to expand.

The problem for the Spanish was it also introduced successful revolts. Gaspar Yanga, known as the first liberator of the Americas, led the first successful slave revolt in Mexico in 1570. Gaspar helped establish one of the first Black colonies in the "new world." They were able to live among themselves for nearly 40 years, until the Spanish militia attacked them in 1609.

Using the terrain to their advantage, Gaspar and his followers pushed the Spanish back. They forced the Spanish to agree to Gasper's terms, including freedom and signed a peace treaty in 1618. The town of San Lorenzo de Los Negros was officially recognized as a free Black settlement.

African nations also continued to push back. In the Battle of the

Lucala in 1590, the Matamba and Ndongo armies united to defeat the Portuguese. But the Portuguese didn't give up so easily. They launched attacks on Angola from 1618 to 1622, until Nzinga Mbande was invited to join peace negotiations. Despite signing treaties, the Portuguese didn't keep their word and continued to attack and kidnap people. After Queen Nzinga's brother died, she took over in 1624. Queen Nzinga tried her best to strengthen the peace treaty. She even converted to Christianity, got baptized, and adopted the name Anna. It didn't take her long to learn the hard way, treaties with Europeans don't mean much.

Queen Nzinga was forced to flee by 1626, but she was a warrior who refused to accept defeat. After taking over Matamba, she realized she would have to fight back in a different way. Queen Nzinga built an army by allowing Africans who escaped slavery into her kingdom. She also organized mercenaries who were trained by the Portuguese. She even formed alliances with former rivals, and went as far as marrying the chief of the Imbangala to increase her army.

Queen Nzinga hand-picked soldiers to infiltrate Portuguese armies and get information to attack from the inside. She also used feuds between European nations to her advantage, becoming allies with the Dutch. By always encouraging insurrections and pitting Europeans against each other, Queen Nzinga was able to create an anti-Portuguese coalition. She kept them at bay for decades. When the Portuguese got word of Queen Nzinga's feats, they sent an army to retake the land in 1644, but they were defeated. However, after the Dutch were forced to retreat, the Portuguese sent the largest army Queen Nzinga would ever have to face.

After being defeated in 1648, Nzinga retreated to change strategy. She began using guerrilla warfare tactics to fight a bigger army. She even led troops into battle when she was over the age of 60. Eventually, Queen Nzinga focused more on building her nation into a superpower. By the time she died, Europeans were forced to recognize her as an equal. Queen Nzinga and her father continued the fight against the Portuguese and other colonizers. But with superior weapons, Europeans ultimately gained control.

Portugal and Spain dominated the slave trade until the 1600s. After Elizabeth I died in 1603, her successor, King James took over. Within a year he reached a treaty with Spain, giving the British access to the "new world." The treaty also gave the British access to the papal bulls, collectively known as the Doctrine of Discovery. The British established their first permanent colony in Jamestown, VA, in 1607.

After previous attempts to establish the Jamestown colony failed, the British initially struggled, nearly suffering the same fate. In what was called the starving time, most of them died. Those who survived resorted to cannibalism and boiling leather to drink. With expressions like, "He who does not work, will not eat," the British were on the verge of abandoning Jamestown. However, the natives showed them how to cultivate the land and what they could or couldn't eat. Once they learned to grow their own food and tobacco, they could sustain themselves. More Europeans were sent to the "new world" as indentured servants.

Melanated people have generally always accepted and welcomed Europeans with open arms. Far too often, it has come back to bite them. There's also resistance dating back to 1454 when colonizers reported being attacked by 150 men. Some believed white Christians were bad people who ate the flesh of people they kidnapped. There may even be truth behind it.

Historically, Europeans have always been fascinated with the power of melanin and the culture of the people. Yet, they claimed Negros didn't want their friendship on any terms, only to slaughter them all and sacrifice their possessions to their Gods.

Africans who chose to embrace Europeans traded animals and other goods in exchange for iron, copper, and tobacco. They were often betrayed, and Europeans took more than agreed on. They didn't only use brute force to conquer. One of their main tools is deception, along with the divide-and-conquer technique. To this day, many use talking points like Africans sold other Africans into slavery to justify the barbaric crimes against humanity. However, notice when someone's regurgitating what they've heard, they're never specific about which nation, leader, or tribe was involved, nor the time period. Don't let them get away with it.

Ask yourself, if Europeans sold slaves and became wealthy, Arabs sold slaves and became wealthy, Americans sold slaves and became wealthy, why did Africans sell their own people and lose everything? By

1610, the Portuguese had already turned the Dahomey kingdom into a slave-trading state. Europeans fought each other for control of slave ports along the coast. They went from nation to nation with superior weapons, threatening to enslave or murder the people if they didn't capture others.

Africans still didn't understand the level of deception they were dealing with. There were cases of Africans selling captives in exchange for weapons for self-defense, but they were only one day away from being tricked and kidnapped themselves. In one case, an African slave trader, Daaga, was tricked into getting on the boat. He was shipped to Cuba where it is said he led his own mutiny.

Like in modern times, I'm sure there were those who'd sell out their own people for whatever reason. An African chief, Ndorkstu, had been trading slaves in exchange for guns and other resources until he found out his relatives were being tricked and kidnapped during the exchanges. Other leaders who traded with Europeans, like Madam Tinubu of Nigeria and King Afonso I of Kongo, realized the inhumane treatment of the people that were taken.

After King Afonso wrote letters to the Portuguese about his concerns, he became a target and was almost assassinated. Many started to resist the slave trade, but it was already too late. Africans realized the people taken away on the big ships weren't coming back. When they heard stories about what was happening to them, many nations tried to fight back but simply lacked the firepower. Not to mention, the Arab slave trade had already been going on for a thousand years.

Religious, political, and tribal differences also made it difficult to overcome language barriers and unify. Once captured, they faced conditions in slave ports so horrible, many died before they were sent away. They were kept in dark dungeons for months at a time, crammed into small spaces in chains, forced to defecate on themselves and each other. This behavior may have been normal in European society, but was unheard of and unimaginable to the natives and Africans. Many people killed themselves and their children because the ancestors knew that death was better than bondage.

CHAPTER 2.
1619: THE CASUAL KILLING ACT

When "20 and odd Negroes" landed near Jamestown in 1619, many marked it as the beginning of slavery in North America. Of course, both free and enslaved Africans were already here. Many choose 1619 because the British created the thirteen colonies.

There's a common misnomer that the first Africans brought into the colonies were slaves. However, when they arrived, they were labeled and sold as indentured servants. There's a huge difference between slavery for life and indentured servitude—just ask the Irish.

Indentured servants only worked for a period, then were released and paid dues. As brutal as Europeans were, they still abided by the Doctrine of Discovery, somewhat following the rules of slavery. If you were Christianized and accepted the ways of the Englishman, you could earn your freedom and maybe even acquire land.

Many of the first Africans to arrive were already Christianized and given European names. It's important to note, unlike many Europeans who agreed to come to the "new world" as servants, Africans didn't choose to come of their own free will. Antoney and Isabella Negro were among the first "20 and odd Negroes" who arrived. They eventually gave birth to a son, William Tucker, becoming the first African family on record in the colony.

Black and white servants were treated as relatively equal at the time. Still, by 1639, Virginia passed a law specifically excluding Negros from the right to arm themselves with weapons. Despite the myth of the African savage, slavery and indentured servitude weren't based solely on race. But things quickly changed for the worse.

In 1640, a Dutchman named Victor, a Scotsman named James, and an African named John Punch tried to escape servitude under a wealthy planter named Hugh Gwyn. All three were caught and sent back to Virginia. They were sentenced to receive lashes and pay dues for any losses incurred. Victor and James were ordered to serve an additional four years in servitude.

However, John Punch was sentenced to serve Gwyn for the rest of his natural life. Essentially, he became the first slave on record in the British colonies.

This was the first significant difference in treatment based on race in the American court system, and we've been disproportionately impacted ever since. In 1641, Mathias De Sousa became the only person of African descent elected to colonial Maryland's General Assembly, despite arriving as an indentured servant.

The Pilgrims didn't land on Plymouth Rock until 1620. They were the outcasts and criminals of England. When they arrived, most of the Indigenous population had already died out from violence and diseases brought by Europeans. The few who remained welcomed the Pilgrims with open arms.

The natives introduced them to their culture and treated them like family. They showed them what they could eat, how to fish, and how to cultivate the land. By the next year, the harvest was so successful, the Pilgrims and natives feasted for three days, giving birth to the myth of Thanksgiving.

Before the Pilgrims landed, they signed the Mayflower Compact. They agreed to follow English law but self-govern themselves separately from the Virginia Colony. The Virginia Colony was founded for economic reasons and consisted mostly of men. The Plymouth colony was comprised of more women and families. Pilgrims were escaping religious persecution themselves and preached the Bible more than anyone. Yet, they were the first to legalize slavery officially in Massachusetts in 1641.

In 1642, Virginia passed laws to distinguish Black women from all other women.

Multiple statutes required every youth, 16 and up, to pay taxes, including Negro women. All other women were exempt, regardless of age. Laws like these made it more difficult for Black women to find partners. When Black women married, their husbands were forced to pay more taxes. Despite the odds, the first Black marriage on record took place in New Amsterdam in 1641.

But Virginia was just getting started. In 1642, they passed one of the first Fugitive Slave Laws in the colonies. Anyone who helped a slave escape was fined in pounds of tobacco. The second time a slave was caught trying to escape, they branded the slave with the letter R. The New England Confederation adopted their own Fugitive Slave Laws in 1643. However, slavery wasn't legalized in Connecticut until 1650. Not to be outdone, the Dutch introduced new rules regarding slavery in New Netherlands. They required ex-slaves to give fixed amounts of their crops to the Dutch West India Company after being freed. Rhode Island was one of the few places to pass laws restricting slavery. It was forbidden for anyone to be enslaved for more than 10 years, but the law was rarely enforced.

As race-based slavery in the colonies took shape, there is a false notion that the first slave owner in America was Black. While Anthony Johnson may have been the first Black slave owner on record, his case wasn't decided until 15 years after John Punch was sentenced.

Anthony arrived from Angola in 1621. He was one of the few who survived, despite diseases and wars with the natives, including the Powhatan Attack of 1622. Eventually, he earned his freedom, acquired land, and adopted the name Anthony Johnson.

As one of the few landowners in Virginia of any race, Anthony purchased both Black and white indentured servants. After his plantation burned down in 1653, a court agreed to exempt Anthony and his wife Mary from paying taxes for the rest of their lives. The court's ruling was in direct defiance of a statute requiring all free Negro men and women to pay taxes to the crown. Most Africans weren't getting the land they were promised.

In 1654, Anthony's neighbor, Robert Parker, convinced a servant named John Casor to run away. Parker told John he was being illegally detained and he'd help him escape. When Anthony found out, he sued Parker and John Casor for his return. Parker was a white planter himself, and initially, the court ruled in his favor. But after an appeal in 1655, the court reversed the decision. Parker was ordered to pay dues to Anthony, and John Casor was returned, despite arguing his contract was expired.

Anthony Johnson's story was unique for several reasons. While he wasn't the only Black landowner, he was likely seen as a Black Englishman. Not only did he live in a small window in American history where race wasn't the biggest issue, unlike other free Africans, the courts also ruled in his favor. However, within a few years, racism became a systematic institution. Anthony and his family were forced to move to Maryland. When he died in 1670, an all-white jury ruled that Anthony's land and property, including his servants, could be seized by the state.

They said, because he was a Negro and by consequence an alien, he wasn't entitled to the same rights as whites. The 50 acres of land Anthony left his family was given to his neighbor's son George Parker, although his son Richard lived there for five years.

In the North, the Pilgrims had already passed race-based laws by 1656. Massachusetts prohibited Negros from arming themselves or training in the militia, reversing a statute from four years earlier. New Hampshire and New York soon followed. Connecticut also banned free Negros from joining the militia by 1660. Although Pilgrims led the way in legalizing slavery, the Virginia colony passed laws that created the basis for chattel slavery and modern race relations.

The first anti-miscegenation law was passed in Virginia in 1661. The statute said, "If any white Christian commits fornication with a Negro man or woman," they'd be fined. By 1662, Virginia enacted the hereditary law. Every child born to an enslaved woman inherited the status of the mother. There is a reason colonizers went against the English and Biblical law of "you are what your father is." It allowed them to still have sexual access to Black women and enslave their own children.

If a Negro woman under an indentured contract produced a child with the owner, consensual or not, they were forced to serve an additional two years. Although these laws mostly affected white males and Black women relations, white women weren't exempt. When white women were caught sleeping with a Black man, they were fined heavily. If they couldn't afford to pay the fine, they were forced into servitude.

By 1663, a Maryland law presumed all Africans coming into the colony were slaves.

Any free European woman married to an African man lost their freedom as well. If any children were produced, they were automatically considered slaves. Basically, if either of your parents were Black, you were born enslaved. South Carolina began granting slave owners twenty acres of land for every male slave and ten acres for every female slave they brought into the colony.

Meanwhile, in Gloucester County, VA, the first documented slave revolt in the colonies took place in 1663. The Gloucester Conspiracy, aka the Birkenhead Rebellion, was the first time African, Native, and European servants attempted to unite against their enslavers. They armed themselves and planned to march to the governor's mansion to demand freedom. If the governor resisted, they'd threaten to use violence and take freedom by any means. Before they got to the governor, a Black servant named John Birkenhead informed authorities. Many of them were captured and beheaded. As a reward, Birkenhead received five pounds of tobacco and his freedom, although it probably didn't help him or his descendants in the long run.

By 1664, Virginia made a clear distinction between European servants and Africans facing perpetual servitude. Virginia began to make Negro synonymous with slave. Soon, New York, New Jersey, the Carolinas, and Maryland followed suit. Maryland also enacted a law forbidding marriage between white women and Black men.

As much blood as Europeans spilled, they still followed the Doctrine of Discovery. But in 1667, Virginia passed a law to ensure baptizing Negros wouldn't save them from bondage. Albeit rare, before this law, Black people could be granted freedom if they proved to the court they'd accepted the ways of the Englishman and were baptized. Elizabeth Key Grinstead was one of the few to win a freedom suit. Elizabeth's father, Thomas Key, was an Englishman, but her mother was enslaved. Although Key denied being Elizabeth's father, he was charged and convicted. Key was a member of the Virginia House of Burgess and was forced to support her. After baptizing Elizabeth, he arranged for apprenticeships to teach her skills.

After Key died, Elizabeth was sold to John Mottram. When Elizabeth's indenture ended, Mottram refused to let her go for years. Mottram eventually brought in more servants, including William Grinstead. Elizabeth and William married and had a child but when Mottram died, Elizabeth was listed as a Negro and faced being sold again. Grinstead was a white lawyer and convinced her to file a freedom suit for her and their son. She argued she was the daughter of a white man and a Christian, thus it was against English law to enslave her. She won her freedom, but within a few years, others weren't so lucky.

By the late 1660s, England enacted stricter laws on enslaved Africans in the colonies. Slaves were forbidden from leaving the plantation without a pass, and never on Sunday. They were prohibited from owning weapons. Slaves were even forbidden from owning horns, whistles, or anything they could use to send messages. To make matters worse, Virginia passed the Casual Killing Act in 1669. Many feel it's still in effect in policing today.

The Casual Killing Act declared, "If any slave resist his master (or other by his master's order correcting him), and by the extremity of the correction should chance to die, that his death shall not be accompted felony, but the master (or that other person appointed by the master to punish him) be acquit from molestation, since it cannot be assumed that malice (which alone makes murder a felony) should induce any man to destroy his own estate." It also legalized raping enslaved Black women. They didn't assume that was malicious either.

To solidify the new race-based laws, in 1670, Virginia passed legislation to enslave all non-Christians (non-whites) who arrived by ship. In addition, free Negros and natives were forbidden from owning any white Christian servants. Many say the Casual Killing Act was created to protect white women and their cruel treatment of slaves, including enslaved children.

Not to be outdone, the Pilgrims in Massachusetts passed a law as sick as it was cruel and devastating to the Black family. Perhaps for the first time in history, a law was passed allowing children to be separated from their families and sold. Many Pilgrims in Massachusetts came from Barbados and the West Indies, bringing their slave codes with them. The so-called Puritans pushed the bible while preaching melanated people weren't human and were inferior. Most Pilgrims that came to the colonies brought that mindset with them.

By 1661, the slave codes in Barbados denied Black people the most basic human rights. The law stated, "If any Negro or slave whatsoever shall offer any violence to any Christian by striking or any other form of violence, such Negro or slave shall for his or her first offense be severely whipped by the Constable." For the second offense, they'd slit their noses and burn part of their face with an iron. Other codes ensured Negros wouldn't get a legal trial with a jury of their peers. The law referred to Negros as "heathenish, brutish, and dangerous."

The Royal African Company dominated the slave trade in North America for nearly a half-century. Originally created in 1660, in 1672, King Charles II restructured the company and issued a new charter. His charter gave the British the right to occupy land, maintain troops, and exercise martial law in West Africa. Their goal was to obtain silver, gold, and human beings to enslave. By the 1680s, the Royal African Company trafficked nearly 5,000 people from Africa to the "new world" annually.

As more slaves arrived, Virginia decided to double down on the Casual Killing Act in 1672. The law allowed the slave patrol, aka patty rollers, to wound or kill any Black person resisting arrest. The law also stated since slaves were property, anyone who injured or killed a slave while arresting them had to compensate the owner. In a way, it gave them more protection than we have today. The Pilgrims in Massachusetts wanted to keep up with the competition. In 1673, they passed another law, this time attacking Black economics. White Christians were forbidden from engaging in commerce or trading with Negros, free or enslaved.

The groundwork for racism was officially established. As the slave codes were introduced into the colonies, the Black population increased. In 1625, there were twenty-three Black people documented in Virginia. In 1648, there were three hundred. By 1675, the Black population in Virginia rose to five thousand. Most kidnapped Africans were taken to the Caribbean. In the West Indies, the slave population grew to about 100,000.

European immigrants chose to come to the "new world" as indentured servants, but they weren't quite getting what were promised either. In 1676, Nathaniel Bacon led a revolt that ended with Jamestown burning to the ground. Some say Bacon's Rebellion was about class, and in a way, it was. For Nathaniel Bacon it wasn't, but he used classism to unite the people. Bacon himself was born to wealthy parents. They paid his way into Cambridge, allowing him to study law. His parents even financed a trip for him to get across the Atlantic.

Once Bacon arrived in Virginia, he appointed himself to the governor's council but was rejected. He and Governor William Berkley were at odds over how they should handle issues with Indigenous tribes. Bacon didn't care how the rich treated the poor, or what was happening to Negros. The revolt began because Bacon wanted to kill more "Indians," but the governor didn't want a war.

Bacon convinced poor white and Black men to unite, leading them to slaughter Indigenous tribes. When the governor found out, he demanded they stop the attacks. Instead, Bacon led them to the governor's doorstep as they set fire to Jamestown. He was doing well, leading a successful rebellion, but then, he died of diarrhea. After Bacon's death, the rebellion was over. Bacon's Rebellion was one of the first successful rebellions uniting both Blacks and whites.

The revolt resulted in the ruling class ending the indentured servant "headright" system. Instead, they looked for ways to keep the poor from ever uniting again. Virginia passed multiple laws, one of which forbid all Negros, free or enslaved, from carrying firearms. Slaves were required to have a pass anytime they left the plantation and were restricted from gathering in a group, including at funerals. Anyone who violated the law received twenty lashes on their bare back.

Virginia mandated harsher punishments for slaves who tried to escape or assault a white person. Self-defense by any Negro against any white Christian was completely outlawed by 1682. If a Black person defended themselves against anyone white, it was punishable by thirty lashes up to death.

The Dutch passed a series of slave codes between 1682-1685. Starting with Black economics, they outlawed engaging in commerce or trade with Negros. It was illegal for slaves to sell or trade goods. Negros and Indigenous people were forbidden from carrying firearms or meeting in groups. The Quakers started to speak out against slavery in Pennsylvania in 1688. The first known organized protest against slavery was a written petition, but only four people signed it.

Although some "good" white people have always been against racism, many more have been for it. By 1690, every English colony sanctioned slavery. In South Carolina, the British introduced the "Act for the Better Ordering of Slaves" from Barbados. The act called for corporal punishment against slaves, including branding, nose slitting, and other emasculating punishments. It also required slaves to get written permission before leaving the plantation.

The slave codes were designed to protect the few white elites from the growing slave population. It also prevented poor whites from uniting with Negros by putting them in a higher social class. Europeans witnessed the treatment of melanated people and realized the advantages of having white skin in the system being created. Even worse, they started enjoying those privileges.

CHAPTER 3.
THE DOOR OF NO RETURN:
SIGNS OF INSURRECTIONS

For the first time in history, a group of people was subjugated based on skin color. The gift of melanin was designed to protect us, especially from the sun. But it was being used against us. Melanated people saw they'd have to unify to fight back.

In Westmoreland, VA, the first all-Black slave revolt was organized in 1687. However, it was over before it started. A European servant named Nicholas Spencer heard about the revolt and informed the governor. They executed everyone they believed to be involved. The next year, a slave named Sam was charged and convicted of "promoting a Negroe Insurrection in the Colony" without evidence. They whipped Sam and everyone involved. Since Sam was allegedly the leader, they ordered him to wear a heavy iron collar on his neck for the rest of his life. If he ever took it off or set foot off the plantation, he was to be hung.

The governor's council complained slaves were given too much freedom. They warned planters about letting them out on the weekends. Guilt and fear of retribution led to stricter laws and harsher penalties to prevent any evil ideas of freedom. Undeterred, in 1691, a slave named Mingoe managed to escape. Mingoe convinced a large group of rebels to attack plantations throughout Virginia. They took livestock, guns, and other weapons, using anything they could find to destroy plantations in three counties. Most of the damage occurred in Middlesex and Rappahannock counties before it ended.

There were at least 84 recorded rebellions in Virginia alone. In response, Virginia passed laws to create a systematic plan to catch runaway slaves in 1691. Slave owners were given the right to receive compensation if a slave was killed while being captured. If a slave owner freed someone, they were responsible for transporting the Negro out of the colony within six months. Virginia also passed a series of laws forbidding marriage between Europeans and Negros.

If a European married a Negro or mulatto, they were forced to leave the colony within three months. English women who gave birth to mulatto babies were fined 15 pounds of tobacco. If they were unable to pay within a month, they were forced to serve five years in servitude. Additionally, children with white mothers and Black fathers were forced to serve a thirty-year indenture. Many times, they were enslaved for life. Virginia also denied slaves the right to a jury trial and prohibited them from owning horses, cattle, hogs, or any pets.

Meanwhile, South Carolina finally figured out how to cultivate rice in 1694, increasing the demand for slaves. Within two years, the Royal African Company lost its monopoly. By 1700, the righteous Pilgrims in Pennsylvania had legalized and regulated slave trading.

Delaware, previously under Pennsylvania law, became its own colony in 1701. Delaware kept the same slave codes, including the Act of 1700. This allowed for harsher punishments for resisting, including whippings, castration, and even death. If a Negro, free or enslaved, was accused of a crime, they'd be tried in a non-jury court. If a white woman accused them of rape, it was punishable by death. Negros were also forbidden from arming themselves or meeting together in groups of four or more without permission.

New Amsterdam, now New York, passed similar laws. Slaves were forbidden from gathering in groups of more than three. Anyone who disobeyed received forty lashes. Slavers could discipline them however they chose, aside from cutting off limbs or killing them. Slaves were also prohibited from engaging in trade or testifying against Europeans in court. Since the 1680s, New Amsterdam had laws forbidding Europeans and free Negroes from selling liquor to slaves, accepting their goods or money, or allowing them to visit their homes.

By 1703, New Amsterdam required slave owners to pay at least fifty pounds of tobacco for each slave they freed, claiming freed slaves would become a public nuisance. Slavers in the North feared an uprising; after all, slaves were created to do what they physically couldn't. A Connecticut law assigned the punishment of whipping to any slaves who disturb the peace or assault whites. Negros, apprentices, and servants were also prohibited from drinking in taverns and inns without permission. However, Connecticut required slave owners to pay for care for elderly and disabled slaves. In Rhode Island, laws were passed to restrict even free Negros.

Neither Negros nor Indigenous people could be out at night without a pass. The Virginia Slave Codes of 1705 were another series of laws that shaped the Black experience in America. Free Negros lost the right to run for public office, and all Negros were denied the right to testify as a witness in court. Laws against Negros carrying weapons or physically assaulting Europeans were reinforced. To stop runaways, slaves were restricted from traveling freely without written permission. Any slave caught without a pass and unwilling or unable to name their owner, was arrested and became property of the state. Slaves were also forbidden from serving in the militia.

To top it off, more laws were passed to reenforce anti-miscegenation. If a European married a Negro, freed or enslaved, they'd be forced to serve six months in jail and fined ten pounds of tobacco. Biracial children born to European mothers and Black fathers had their indentures increased even more, although many were already enslaved for life anyway. If a minister married a European and a Negro, they were fined 10,000 pounds of tobacco.

Maybe more important than any law, the Virginia Slave Codes defined the status of a slave as any non-white Christian. Negros were considered savages and less than animals; therefore, they couldn't be Christian. Essentially, all Africans, natives, and mixed race people in Virginia were considered property, and their owners could kill them as punishment.

Massachusetts also banned marriage and sexual relationships between Negros and Europeans. Of course, this law wasn't enforced since Europeans raped Black people constantly. New York enforced laws to execute certain runaway slaves. By 1706, New York passed a law legalizing the death penalty for any Negro who killed a European. Virginia continued using the threat of an uprising to pass laws to prevent slaves from assembling in 1709. In some cases, the threat was real. But many times, people were charged and convicted before anything happened. On

Easter Sunday, in 1710, another all-Black revolt was supposed to take place.

However, a slave named Will betrayed them and told authorities. In exchange, Will was granted freedom and received forty pounds of tobacco.

White guilt and the fear of rebellious Negros led to complaints about the presence of so many slaves. In response, New York passed a law in 1711 stating, "All Negroe and native slaves were to be hired at the Market House at the Wall Street Slip." The first official market for selling and trading human beings gave birth to the Wall Street stock exchange.

The slave population in New York fought against oppression from the beginning. In 1708, four slaves killed at least seven Europeans during an uprising in Long Island. However, all four slaves were executed. Many say the first successful rebellion was the New York Slave Revolt of 1712. It started after 23 slaves armed themselves with guns, knives, and any weapons they could find. After setting businesses, homes, and other buildings on fire, they killed every white firefighter who showed up. They killed at least nine whites, causing panic to spread.

Every Negro male who was at least 14 was arrested and questioned about the attack. The witch hunt led to seventy arrests. Twenty-seven people were charged, and twenty-one were convicted and sentenced to death. They burned twenty alive, before executing the last person on a breaking wheel in public to send a message.

After the revolt, New York strengthened laws against Negros carrying weapons or congregating in groups. Free Negros were also restricted from owning or inheriting land. Melanated people could no longer build generational wealth by passing land down to their children. Many slaves in New York attempted to escape to Canada. But in 1715, New York legalized the execution of any slave caught 40 miles north of Albany. Rhode Island also legalized slavery that year.

As the demand for slaves continued to increase, Britain dominated the slave trade. With the help of European Jews, the Dutch weren't far behind. Centuries before the slave trade, European Jews were cast out of England. Many ended up in the Netherlands. By the 1630s, European Jews became heavily involved in slave trading in the "new world." The Dutch West

India Company eventually took control of Brazil from Portugal. Close to 1,500 European Jews moved to Brazil by 1654. When Portugal regained control, many European Jews had already acquired sugar plantations and mills. More importantly, they had created a system for buying and selling humans on credit. Essentially, European Jews became the first slave creditors and played a major role in expanding the slave trade.

After leaving Brazil, many came to New Amsterdam and dominated the slave trade.

Those who chose to remain in Holland received a charter from the Dutch West India Company permitting them to colonize the "wild coast." Settlers with more slaves paid fewer taxes.

Between 1658-1674, the Dutch West India Company, which included the Jewish, were responsible for at least 24,555 kidnapped Africans being sent to the "new world," about 55 percent of the total. Europeans were in a constant battle over land and control of the slave trade until 1713. After England won the war, European nations created the Treaty of Utrecht, which gave England exclusive rights to ship kidnapped Africans to Spanish colonies in the "new world." It also laid the groundwork for Europeans to stop fighting each other and establish a code against us.

As human trafficking increased, in 1715, Maryland declared, "All Negroes entering into the colony, and all their future descendants will be slaves for life." New York also passed harsher Fugitive Slave Laws. In Louisiana, the French began shipping in slaves in 1716, and by 1718, New Orleans was established. Within a few years, the city had more slaves than free Europeans. Since South Carolina also had a higher slave population, they limited voting to free white male landowners in 1721. But in 1724, the French brought the Code Noir from the Caribbean to New Orleans. Saint- Domingue, under French rule, was described as one of the most brutal colonies for slaves.

The Code Noir forced all slaves to convert and be baptized in the Roman Catholic Church. Any other religion was forbidden. If owners allowed slaves to practice their original spiritual beliefs, they were also punished. Additionally, slaves were prohibited from marrying without permission, and their children still inherited their mother's status. They were forbidden from carrying weapons, except to hunt and only with permission. Furthermore, slaves were prohibited from selling goods and forbidden from selling sugar cane completely. They were also forbidden from gathering under any circumstances.

If a slave hit his owner, their wife, or their children, the slave was executed. If a fugitive slave was gone for more than a month, their ears were cut off and they were branded for the first offense. After the second offense, their hamstrings were cut, and they were branded again. If there was a third time, they'd be executed. If a free Negro provided refuge for a slave, they were beaten by the owner and fined three hundred pounds of sugar for every day they provided shelter.

The Code Noir also included laws requiring owners to provide clothes and food for slaves. They were further forced to provide for the old and the sick, who were often neglected. If an owner accused a slave of a crime they didn't commit and killed them, they were fined.

Although they didn't get fair trials, slaves were allowed to testify, but only for information. Still, they could chain and beat slaves as they saw fit, excluding torture and mutilation.

More importantly, the slave codes forbade prepubescent enslaved children from being sold separately or taken away from their parents. Children born into slavery were automatically owned by the slaver's wife. If an owner raped and impregnated a slave, he was fined and the children were taken away from him, although they remained in bondage. Unlike other slave codes, the Code Noir still allowed owners to free their slaves if they chose.

The French, Dutch, Spanish, Portuguese, and English all had different methods and laws for slavery. Yet, all were just as cruel as the next. Most Europeans came to the "new world" as poor criminals escaping persecution. Europe wasn't sending its best people. They slaughtered anyone they believed was planning a revolt, and every rumor led to stricter laws.

In 1727, a revolt involving free and enslaved Negros and people of mixed race was allegedly set to take place. In the beginning, it was clear where biracial people stood. Although the revolt was unsuccessful, there wasn't enough evidence to convict anyone. However, anyone suspected of being involved was shipped out of Virginia, and their owners were reimbursed for the loss of property. After the alleged uprising, Virginia passed more laws denying free Blacks the right to vote or own guns. They also increased the number of slave patrols.

Still, Negros continued to fight back. The Chesapeake Rebellion of 1730 was supposedly the largest insurrection up to that time. However, white planters quickly suppressed it with the help of native tribes including the Pasquotank Indians and possibly the Cherokee. It started after rumors spread that King George I of England freed any slave that had been baptized. Although it was just a rumor, nearly 200 slaves gathered in Princess Anne County, VA, and elected their own leaders. They planned to attack on a Sunday in October while whites were in church. Many of them were arrested and at least 29 people were hanged. However, many escaped into an area known as the Great Dismal Swamp where some lived for generations.

By 1730, European indentures and non-Black Indian slavery were coming to an end. In some peace treaties tribes like the Cherokee agreed to the fugitive slave clause and often returned runaways. As the number of enslaved negros continued to rise, between 1730 and 1750, the number of African women brought to the "new world" started to balance out for the first time. Slaves made up a fourth of the population in Virginia. As the number of slaves increased, so did white fear.

The governor, William Gooch, called in the militia to investigate slave conspiracies. Every slave caught off the plantation was arrested and many were whipped. Gooch hoped it would convince them to accept slavery and "rest happy with their condition because perpetual slavery was the best thing for them."

Six months later, another conspiracy was reported after Negros dared to assemble while Europeans were at church. Before their plan was discovered, they elected a leader. However, after they were caught, four were executed, and the rest were punished severely. When the governor found out the plan had gotten as far as Norfolk county, he ordered the militia to patrol two or three times a week. Gooch deputized untrained farmers and planters to prevent any night or Sunday meetings. He said, "Every European male should bring his firearm to church so they wouldn't get caught off guard."

But the resistance wasn't only in Virginia, in Louisiana, there was also the Samba Rebellion of 1731. Samba was said to have been involved in several rebellions after he was captured in Senegal, including a revolt which led to the French losing Fort Arguin in Mauritania. Even while being transported to Louisiana he is said to have planned a revolt but was discovered after he was betrayed. According to the writing of his enslaver Antoine Simon Lepage Du Pratz, he overheard about plans of an insurrection during an argument between an enslaved woman and a French marine after he slapped her for disobeying him.

Du Pratz claimed while investigating he overheard Samba and several others planning to kill all whites in the area and take over. Within two days, eight men including Samba, and one woman was arrested. They were tortured for nearly a week until several of them confessed but Samba never said a word. A few hours after the confession all eight men were killed on a breaking wheel and the woman was hung.

While the British were busy instituting slavery, in 1731, Spanish Florida offered slaves freedom if they could make it there, reversing a law from the previous year requiring slave to be returned. However, they were only considered free if they converted to Roman Catholicism.

Otherwise, they were sent back to their enslaver or sold. As slaves fought to get to Florida, many revolts took place on slave ships. In 1732, enslaved people took over a vessel sailing from New Hampshire. They killed the captain John Majors of Portsmouth, NH, and his crew before taking the cargo and abandoning the ship. There was also the Little George Ship revolt in 1730.

So many successful revolts took place on slave ships, we'll never know about all of them. Between the late 1400s and early 1700s, hundreds of slave forts were built on the Gold Coast. Before kidnapped Africans were shipped to the "new world," the dehumanizing process began in those dungeons. Up to 1,000 male and 500 female victims of all ages were shackled together and crammed into small spaces without ventilation. They were always kept in the dark, not only to keep them lost and confused, but to break them down psychologically. They were crammed into spaces so small they couldn't lie down. There was no sanitation, and feces, blood, and any other human waste you could imagine covered the floor. Not to mention the odor. Many people got sick and died from these conditions alone.

Of course, men and women were kept separately. Europeans constantly raped helpless women and little girls of all ages. Anyone showing signs of rebelling was kept in small confinement cells, isolated in the dark, similar to the hole in prison today. The point wasn't to kill, since they needed slaves, but to fully dehumanize them. After being held in these spaces for months, they were shipped off, never to return home again. That's why they called it the "door of no return."

Slave ships were redesigned so they could traffic as many humans as possible. Slaves, including pregnant women, were shackled and stacked on top of one another and stuffed into spaces so small they couldn't move. Conditions were so bad many attempted suicide, but Europeans did everything they could to stop them. They were chained together, so if one went overboard, anyone connected did as well. Those who managed to free themselves often jumped overboard. Most of them ended up drowning to avoid being caught.

When slaves refused to eat, they were met with threats against them or their loved ones, if not flat-out violence. If they became weak, injured, or sick, they were thrown overboard. So many people died en route, sharks changed their migration patterns to follow the slave trail.

Once they arrived at whatever European colony they were sent to, the dehumanizing process continued. The people were branded, stripped, and inspected as if they were goods in a store. The Danish entered the slave trade in 1657. By 1718, they were in control of Saint John in the Virgin Islands. The Danes tried to use prisoners to work the land in the beginning, but they were inadequate. They decided to increase their role in human trafficking, calling slaves Black gold.

Some African nations profited from the European slave trade. The Akwamu tribe began dealing with the Danish, receiving guns and rum for capturing other tribes. Often, we overlook factors that played a role in certain tribes capturing others, such as threats of loved ones being enslaved or killed. However, the Akwamu tribe was known for being harsh with prisoners they conquered from other tribes, although not as cruel as Europeans. In 1730, their king died, weakening the nation and ending their reign as a power in the area. The Akwamu attacking tribes caused tension and animosity with the surrounding nations. As punishment, many were sold to the same Danish people they were doing business with. They saw firsthand, Europeans had no allegiances; they were into making slaves, not friends.

Hundreds of the Akwamu, including their royalty, like King June, King Bolombo, Prince Akashi, and others, were sent to St John. By 1733, the enslaved population in St John outnumbered Europeans 1,087 to 206. Most plantation owners lived in St. Thomas and hired overseers to run their plantations. As the slave population grew, so did European paranoia. Not all rebellions were obvious acts of aggression; most of the time, it was subtle. Africans and indigenous tribes used their knowledge of nature and herbology to their advantage. Enslaved women poisoned owners and overseers as they prepared their food. It was so hard to detect because symptoms were similar to natural diseases. Therefore, poison became the leading cause of death for Europeans.

Whether they were poisoned or died from diseases, European deaths were usually blamed on slaves. In response, St. John passed harsher laws to scare the enslaved, attempting to make them more obedient. Anyone found guilty of poisoning a slave owner or overseer received three pinches from a red-hot pincer, then was placed on the breaking wheel. If an enslaved person knew of another's plan to run away and didn't inform authorities, they were burned on the forehead and received 100 lashes. Any slave caught running away had their leg or ear cut off and received 150 lashes. If any Negro, free or enslaved, harmed or attempted to strike a European, they were hung. Even if a European asked for them to be pardoned, they still chopped off their right hand.

These new slave codes didn't stop the Akwamu people from fighting back. They saw themselves as wealthy merchants, nobles, leaders, and, more importantly, as free. Led by King June, they continued with their plans to revolt. To send a message, the first slaver they retaliated against had a close relationship with the governor who passed the slave codes. At the same time, slaves making a routine delivery of firewood at the Fort at Coral Bay secretly armed themselves with knives used to cut sugar cane. They killed all but one of the Danish soldiers, then raided the fort for guns, ammunition, and other supplies.

The rebels fired one of the Danish cannons, signaling the beginning of the revolution. Normally, the Danes used the cannon as a signal to meet in case of an emergency. But in this case, the rebels used it to ambush them. It was clear they were smart and skilled warriors, killing as many slavers as they could. Women were also involved in the rebellion. A woman named Breffu led one of the groups. The Akwamu slave revolt of 1733 was one of the first relatively successful slave revolts. They took control of St. John, forcing Europeans to flee the island. St. John became the first independent Black state in 1733. Unfortunately, the Akwamu created many rivalries after selling most of the slaves in St. John.

Eventually, they made a deal with the "Free Negroe Core." They offered freedom and money to anyone willing to join the first line of defense. The next year, three European countries joined forces to regain control of the island. Hundreds of French and Swiss troops were sent in with weapons but were unable to compete with rebels they labeled subhuman. The French were forced to send in reinforcements and additional weapons.

The Akwamu were no match against superior weapons and were eventually defeated. Every rebel they captured was executed by hanging, burning, dismemberment, etc. After being cornered, the last rebel groups killed themselves instead of going back into bondage. The revolt lasted for 10 months, fueling the fire for freedom even more.

CHAPTER 4.
AMERICAN REVOLUTION: THE ILLUSION OF WHITENESS

Anytime a revolt happens, the news spreads quickly, along with fear— especially in places where slaves outnumbered Europeans. South Carolina passed a law forcing free Negros to leave the colony in 1735. The law also required the enslaved to wear certain clothes, identifying them as slaves. After Georgia was founded in 1733 by James Oglethorpe, slavery was completely banned in the colony. To Oglethorpe, banning slavery wasn't about being moral, and he wasn't against slavery itself. For him, it was more for political, social, and economic reasons.

Spanish Florida promised slaves freedom in exchange for joining their army and accepting Roman Catholicism. The English knew slaves in Georgia would escape to Florida and help the Spanish. But Georgia quickly realized they couldn't produce nearly half as much without Negros. Without slaves, they could never build wealth.

In French colonies, King Louis XV declared any child born to an enslaved woman and free man could not be sold, furthermore, they'd be granted freedom after a certain time. The law was mostly to stop white slavers from impregnating Black women. But the law impacted a woman's decision on who to reproduce with to ensure her children's freedom.

By 1738, the first Black settlement of free Negros and runaway slaves was established in Florida called Fort Mose. While the Spanish offered slaves freedom and land, Georgia's trustees allowed slaves to be imported into the territory. The next year, South Carolina passed the Security Act. The act required all Europeans to carry firearms seven days a week, including to church on Sundays. One of their biggest fears was an uprising on a Sunday, while they were in church, because slaves didn't work and could easily gather unnoticed.

One Sunday in September 1739, their fears came true. The tension between the English in Georgia and South Carolina, and Spanish Florida, plus the slaves' ambition to be freed, led to the Stono Rebellion. During harvest times, captives were worked harder and treated worse. But they outnumbered Europeans two to one after many of them died from diseases. A man named Jemmy from Angola led the revolt, organizing 20 men by the Stono River. They were fed up and broke into a gun store to arm themselves. They marched through the town with drums, chanting liberty, and killing slave owners and overseers. Most colonies in the "new world" forbade drums for this very reason. Drums were also forbidden to prevent slaves from using them to communicate.

These freedom fighters went from plantation to plantation, killing European men, women, and children. About 25 Europeans were killed, most of them beheaded. They freed and recruited as many people as they could, and by noon, the group grew to 50 or 60. They were about 30 miles from freedom when the militia caught up with them. When the battle ensued, the rebels were outgunned, and many of them were killed. A few escaped; however, all but one were eventually found. Some were executed by decapitation, and the rest were deported to Jamaica.

When Jemmy was captured, he and another leader of the rebellion were decapitated. Their heads were placed on poles along highway US17 in Charleston to send a message.

In response, South Carolina passed the Negro Act of 1740. The first thing the act did was limit the importation of slaves. It wasn't for moral reasons, but they realized those born into slavery were far less rebellious than those who had known freedom. The act also strengthened laws restricting slaves' ability to earn money, gather in groups, or walk around alone. It was also illegal for slaves to grow their own food, and it allowed owners to kill captives they deemed rebellious. The Act of 1740 was the first law prohibiting education, making it illegal to teach enslaved people how to write. They understood how powerful knowledge is, and one thing they've always been afraid of is an educated Black person.

South Carolina required one heavily armed European for every 10 Negros on a plantation. They also started a Christian school, forcing slaves to learn the doctrine of serving their masters. Although they were forbidden from learning how to write, and later to read, Europeans allowed them to read certain parts of the Bible about being good slaves.

Behind only South Carolina, New York had the second most slaves of any colony, with one out of every five people being enslaved. Growing paranoia led to the New York Conspiracy of 1741. During the winter, several fires broke out and Europeans were convinced Negroes were responsible. After convening in court, officials decided to blame three enslaved men, Prince, Cuffee, and Caesar, without evidence.

The sole witness was a 16-year-old Irish girl, Mary Burton. Burton ran a bar many slaves frequented. She told authorities about unlawful gatherings of more than three Negros and about her selling them alcohol. Burton testified that enslaved Negros and some poor Europeans planned to burn the city. She said they planned to kill all the white males and take their women, then elect a Negro king. Although her story didn't make sense, her sole testimony was enough to convict Prince and Caesar.

The owner of the bar, John Hughson Burton, was also convicted of conspiracy. After Mary Burton testified, she was freed from her indenture and paid 100 pounds of tobacco.

Despite their owners testifying in their favor, Prince and Caesar were sentenced to death by being burned at the stake. A day later, another fire broke out. Just because two slaves were in the area, they were immediately burned at the stake. Soon, more accusations by Burton led to around 200 arrests. She may have been the first white girl on record to give false testimony in court that resulted in the death of many Black people, a trend that would continue. Thirty people were sentenced to death by hanging or being burned at the stake. Another 70 were sent to sugar plantations in Barbados as punishment.

Four Europeans were also convicted and executed. The court argued, "A Negroe couldn't come up with a plan like that; it had to be a white person behind it." Seven more whites were expelled from New York, along with any slaves they forced into a false confession.

Anyone refusing to confess was publicly burned at the stake. Once Burton began naming wealthy Europeans, the witch hunt ended, and she was released as a witness. The fires may have been caused by natural conditions during the winter, mixed with unsafe materials they used. In the end, no actual plans for a conspiracy were discovered.

Nevertheless, Virginia made it a felony for slaves to conspire to organize a rebellion, punishable by death. Any enslaved person caught walking around at night was dismembered. If they died, no one was punished. Despite skirmishes with Spanish Florida, Georgia repealed laws outlawing slavery and slave trafficking. On January 1, 1751, Georgia adopted South Carolina's slave codes, with a few changes to ensure Negros wouldn't outnumber Europeans. Once Georgia legalized slavery, the Negro population grew from 500 to 18,000 by 1775.

Most of the people kidnapped from Africa were sent to the Caribbeans. The sugar plantations in places like Jamaica and St-Domingue were known to be the worst plantations of all. By the 1740s, they were the main producers of sugar. Most of the slave codes were developed there, then brought to the colonies. However, in 1751, King George II repealed the Virginia slave codes of 1705, classifying Negros as property.

Meanwhile, in Maryland, a 21-year-old Benjamin Banneker created the first fully functional clock in 1752. By taking apart a pocket watch and studying it, he built the clock using only carved wooden pieces. Benjamin's father was a former slave who'd freed himself and was able to get his own farm. His mother was a free biracial woman, so Benjamin was born free himself. He was self-educated and eventually became an inventor, a mathematician, and an astronomer. He is credited with being the first Black scientist in the colonies, although many were already using science and nature to fight for freedom.

In Mecklenburg, VA, the African Baptist or Bluestone Church was founded on the William Byrd plantation in 1758. The Bluestone Church was the first known Black church, although some say the first Black Baptist Church was founded in Prince George County in 1756. Many used church to practice their own spirituality in secret, but it also served as a place to meet and socialize. Fearing they could plan another revolt, there had to be at least one European present at all times. Religion was another tool used to destroy the minds of slaves.

Europeans used Christianity and the Bible to justify kidnapping and enslaving people, despite escaping religious persecution themselves.

The Quakers in Philadelphia forbade its members from participating in the slave trade.

In 1758, the Quakers even opened a school for free Negro children. They may have been against the institution of slavery, but it doesn't mean they didn't believe in white nationalism and that Negros were subhuman. Benjamin Franklin was among the first to talk about white nationalism, saying, "I'm not British. I'm a white American." In 1751, Franklin wrote, "The Saxons with the English make a principal body of white people on the earth. I wish their numbers were increased. Why increase the sons of Africa, by planting them in America where we have so fair an opportunity of increasing the lovely white and red by excluding all blacks and tawneys?"

Franklin said, "Negroes brought to English sugar plantations greatly diminished whites and hurt poor whites trying to make a living." He also said, "Anyone who acquires new territory, whether it's vacant or he kills/removes enough natives to give his people room, may be called the father of the nation." Many use his white supremacist and white nationalist writings to say he was against slavery, and this is who they call one of the founding fathers.

The last thing they wanted to see was an armed Black man. In 1760, New Jersey forbade slaves from joining the militia. That year, Briton Hammon also wrote A Narrative of the Unknown Sufferings and Surprising Deliverance of Briton Hammon. It was the first autobiographical writing of an enslaved person. The next year, a slave named Jupiter Hammon wrote the first volume of poetry published in the colonies. Despite their achievements, Virginia passed laws to restrict voting to white males in 1762, solidifying the idea of white nationalism.

Europeans fought each other for control of the slave trade and the "new world" for hundreds of years. The British eventually gained the upper hand after the Treaty of Paris was signed, ending the Seven Years' War. The treaty gave Britain all the land occupied by the French east of the Mississippi, except for New Orleans. Essentially, the French were cast out of the "new world," except in Haiti. The British took Florida from Spain, devastating slaves' hopes of acquiring freedom and land.

The natives preferred the French over the British and fought to keep the British out. A war chief named Pontiac, backed by the French, led an uprising known as Pontiac's Rebellion. Some native tribes had already adopted the ways of the Englishmen, with some even enslaving Negros. When King George III issued the Proclamation of 1763, it set aside land for the natives.

Although Europeans were prohibited from colonizing lands west of the Appalachian Mountains, the Proclamation was constantly ignored. When the Indigenous People who fought back started doing damage to the British, word got back to London. The British were forced to send more troops to defend the colony. However, Britain believed if they sent in additional troops, the colonists should pay for it. Britain decided to raise taxes in the colonies to recoup from the war.

The British Parliament passed the Sugar Act in 1764, taxing any products with sugar, including rum. The same group that bought and sold other human beings and separated children from families now felt they were being subjugated because they were taxed for rum. The colonists refused to buy English goods, so the next year, the British passed the Stamp Act. This was the first tax to affect every British colony. They were taxed for every piece of printed paper, including newspapers, licenses, and legal documents, from slave records down to a deck of cards. They were even taxed for the traveling passes slaves were required to have. Of course, free Negros were taxed for the freedom papers they were forced to have.

Britain set up their own courts with judges appointed by the British government. The Act also required colonists to let British soldiers into their homes for rest and shelter at any time.

This led to sayings like "taxation without representation is tyranny," but I guess they didn't think slavery was. The British Parliament eventually repealed the Stamp Act but passed the Declaratory Act in 1766. It gave the British the right to pass any law in the colonies. One of these laws was the Townshend Acts. It imposed taxes on imports like paint, lead, glass, and tea. It also gave British officials the right to search colonizers, their homes, or their businesses at any time, similar to modern stop-and-frisk laws.

At the first Continental Congress, the colonists came up with a multi-colony agreement known as the Non-Importation Agreement. Their goal was to boycott British merchants. Gangs such as the Sons of Liberty led pop-up rebellions. Even British slave merchants were boycotted, essentially ending the slave trade in Philadelphia. Colonists in New York and Boston refused to give British troops shelter. The Massachusetts Assembly was eventually dissolved because they refused to help collect taxes. Likewise, the Virginia House of Burgesses was disbanded after refusing to charge colonists with treason.

The Virginia House of Burgesses condemned British actions. But in the same breath, they reinstated exclusive rights to tax Virginians themselves. Colonists called paying the taxes they owed Britain for their protection oppression while passing tyrannical laws designed to destroy Negros. In 1769, Virginia passed a law stating, "If any slave raped or was accused of raping a white woman, their punishment was castration."

The tension between colonists and Britain continued to rise. There were constant skirmishes until March 1770, when British troops fired into a crowd. In what became known as the Boston Massacre, five people were killed, including a biracial man named Crispus Attucks. Said to be the first victim of the Revolutionary War, Crispus was a runaway slave who made it to Boston. He had gotten involved with a mob of colonists after a British soldier allegedly hit someone at a bar. The colonists used his death for political reasons. After the incident, the British soldiers were arrested and charged.

John Adams, who went on to become the second president, led the defense for the soldiers. Adams made sure to single out Crispus Attucks, arguing his "mad behavior" escalated the conflict. He said, "The Negroe started the mob, and he was armed with a club attacking the soldiers." Adams claimed the soldiers fired in self-defense, fearing for their lives. He may have created the blueprint police use today. He knew that blaming a Black man would win the case, and it did. None of the British soldiers were convicted of murder, and only two were convicted of manslaughter.

The British Parliament ended up repealing all taxes except the tax on tea, but that wasn't enough for the colonists. They didn't want to serve the crown or pay taxes at all. I don't know what it is with Europeans and tea, but in 1773, the British passed the Tea Act. The act gave the British East India Company a monopoly on tea shipped into the colonies. The protest in response resulted in the Boston Tea Party. Colonists dressed as "Indians" and took over British ships. They dumped all the tea in the water, costing Britain a lot of money.

Amid the Boston Tea Party, an enslaved woman named Phillis Wheatley published her book of poems in Boston. It was the first published book written by a Black woman in the "new world." In Silver Bluff, S.C., free and enslaved Negros created their own separate church. Silver Bluff Baptist was co-founded by George Liele, the first Black ordained minister in Georgia. He also trained an enslaved man David George who often went around preaching to other slaves on the plantation. Although David and George left for Nova Scotia after the war, the church is still around today.

After seeing how the colonists responded to the British, many Negros hoped Europeans would realize how evil their practices were. Some even petitioned for their freedom, but were unsuccessful. The Massachusetts General Court didn't think Negros had any natural rights to freedom. However, Britain wanted to put an end to the colonists' disrespect and disloyalty to the crown.

After the Boston Tea Party ended, the British Parliament passed the Coercive Acts. Colonists referred to these laws as the Intolerable Acts. The first law was the Boston Port Act. It shut down the ports in Boston until colonists paid for all the tea they destroyed. Next, they passed the Massachusetts Government Act, taking away any power the government had. Britain replaced government officials with people they appointed. The act also restricted colonists from holding town meetings more than once a year.

The Administration of Justice Act took away the court's power and replaced judges with British ones. Finally, the Quartering Act gave British soldiers the right to move into colonists' homes at any time. Not only that, colonizers had to provide them with food, wash their clothes, and give them a place to sleep. In a society that instituted chattel slavery, they claimed the Intolerable Acts violated the colonial charters and their human rights.

The Continental Congress banned all trading with the British, including slave trading. Connecticut, Rhode Island, Georgia, and Virginia prohibited slaves from being imported completely. They deputized and armed citizens, often referred to as the minutemen, to be ready for the backlash from British soldiers. In the first clash at the Battle of Lexington and Concord, Black minutemen fought on the side of the colonists. However, people like George Washington feared arming Negros, even if they were on his side.

At the age of 11, George Washington inherited 10 slaves from his father. By the 1770s, he had over 150. It is said Washington's dentures were made with teeth brutally ripped from the mouths of slaves. He treated slaves so horribly, they attempted to escape constantly. He feared armed Negros would come for revenge. In 1775, he banned all Negros from joining the militia. However, he took council with certain Negros and listened to their suggestions. He even responded respectfully to a letter sent from Phillis Wheatley.

Although the colonies banned slave trading with Britain, slavery was still legal in every colony, as well as in England. A slave owner in Virginia named William Pitman had a reputation of being so cruel other Europeans constantly took him to court over the way he treated slaves.

After Pitman got drunk, he tied a young boy up by the neck and heels, then brutally beat him with a vine before stomping him to death. Pitman's own children went to the authorities and testified against him. He was so barbaric that, in an unusual case, he was charged, convicted, and sentenced to be hung. It was usually impossible to convict a slave owner since Negros weren't considered human. The law even allowed slaves to be murdered.

Despite Europeans calling Negros nonhuman savages for hundreds of years, in 1775, a German named Johann Friedrich Blumenbach created the modern-day racial classifications.

First, he created the term Caucasian. All Europeans were labeled Caucasian because they came from cold, dark caves in the Caucasus Mountains. Blumenbach incorrectly believed Caucasians were the first race created by God and put here to be over other races. This racially biased "science" helped create the concept of white supremacy many Europeans still hold on to today.

Blumenbach believed other groups degenerated from Caucasians. He labeled Mongolians the yellow race, Malayans the brown race, and

Native Americans the red race. Last was the Ethiopian or the Black race. He considered all Africans Black, except North Africans, because they'd have to admit Black people built great civilizations like Kemet or Egypt.

Blumenbach concluded his studies by stating, Black people weren't inferior and were capable of making healthy decisions. He also said, "There is no savage nation under the sun, and given the right environment, everyone would turn back into white people as they originally were." Although he was clearly wrong, he was right about the Black dominant gene.

Blumenbach was criticized for saying Black people aren't savages. Still, his "work" was the basis for the scientific racism used to justify the inhumane treatment of Black people. Before Blumenbach, a Swedish physician, Carl Linnaeus, also created four different racial groups. He called whites or Europeans "pure and gentle, governed by laws." Linnaeus called Blacks or Africanus, "sly, lazy, and lustful," saying "Black women had no shame." Linnaeus was known as the father of taxonomy to Europeans, using just about every racist stereotype to classify Black people.

Europeans have always used pseudo-science to make racist arguments and disregarded anything that proved them wrong. Anytime Europeans argue about statistics or a study, always ask for the methodology used. The only way they could still call themselves Christians and sleep at night was to tell themselves a lie. If someone repeats that lie enough times, not only will they start believing it, so will we.

CHAPTER 5.
THE AMERICAN CONSTITUTION:
BROKEN PROMISES

From the first war to the last, America has always depended on Black soldiers to defend the same system created to dehumanize them. After George Washington banned Negros from the militia, the British used it to their advantage. The last governor of colonial Virginia, Governor Dunmore, issued a proclamation offering freedom to any slave who fought alongside the British.

He also offered 100 acres of land, plus additional land for each family member.

The proclamation only applied to slaves owned by American "patriots," as Dunmore didn't want to offend white allies. The British returned slaves to owners who were loyal to the crown constantly. Many enslaved people escaped to join the British and quickly gained the upper hand. Nearly 30,000 Black soldiers joined the war. Thomas Jefferson said he lost at least 30 slaves himself. Free Negros joined the British as well because they were subject to many of the same laws and curfews as slaves.

Black soldiers gave the British an advantage. It forced George Washington to recant his statements about arming Negros. Within a few months, Washington was begging Negros to join the militia, despite passing laws against it.

Soon, many Northern colonies were forced to abolish slavery. They offered freedom to any slave who helped them fight. First was Vermont in 1777, then Pennsylvania in 1780, followed by New Hampshire and Massachusetts in 1783. Rhode Island didn't abolish slavery until 1784. Southern colonies refused to offer slaves freedom. Many slavers in the South offered certain enslaved people freedom if they fought bravely for them in the war. But by 1776, nearly 100,000 people escaped bondage and joined the fight for freedom. Many hoped the revolution also applied to them.

As the war raged on, America nominated the white nationalist pedophile, Thomas Jefferson, to draft the Declaration of Independence. In a room full of slaves, these hypocritical criminals presented a document declaring that all men were created equal. While they wrote a document about inalienable rights, both free and enslaved Negros were being deprived of theirs. Still, by 1778, enough Black people made it to Rhode Island to form the first all-Black military unit in America.

That year, a freedman by the name of Paul Cuffe used the revolution to stand up for Black rights. He petitioned the Massachusetts government to either give Black people equal rights under the law or to stop taxing them. He used their argument of "no taxation without representation" against them. Paul was a smart businessman and a Pan-Africanist. By 1811, he was known as the wealthiest Black American and the largest employer of Black workers. He also helped many free and enslaved Black people get to Sierra Leone after the colony was established.

During the 1770s, Paul and his brother John refused to pay taxes because they couldn't vote, and they were briefly jailed. In part, because of their actions, Massachusetts passed a law making every free Negro subject to taxation. However, they weren't granted the same privileges as other citizens, such as the right to vote.

With new hope for freedom, the first Free African Union Society was founded in Newport, RI, in 1780. In 1824, the society changed the name to the Colored Union Church and Society. Since whites controlled all resources, Black people created their own mutual aid societies. They offered cultural and spiritual centers, as well as financial aid to members.

Inspired by the Declaration of Independence, in 1781, a Massachusetts woman named Mum Bett challenged her status as a slave in court. She became the first Black person in Massachusetts to successfully file and win a freedom suit. Once free, she changed her name to Elizabeth Freeman. Although she could not read or write, her story helped influence others to do the same.

The Revolutionary War lasted for eight years, until 1783, formally ending with the Treaty of Paris. The treaty was signed by Benjamin

Franklin, John Adams, Thomas Jefferson, and John Jay. Britain agreed to recognize America as a separate nation. The British remained allies and could trade with America without paying for military protection. However, the treaty gave colonists the right to land west of the Mississippi. But with access to the Northwest Territories, parts of Florida were given back to the Spanish.

With the war over and colonists gaining their independence, America was officially born.

After losing the war, Black soldiers who sided with the British were forced to leave. About 3,000 people in New York alone were sent to Nova Scotia in Canada. The British upheld their promise of freedom, but most of the land grants and supplies they promised went to white loyalists. The few Black people who received anything were given worse land and fewer resources. Some loyalists were even allowed to bring slaves with them.

White loyalists didn't see any difference between free and enslaved Negros and treated them the same. But it allowed many enslaved people to escape by blending in with free Blacks. Black workers were paid a quarter of what whites were paid, although they were often more skilled. Many times, Black workers were the first to be hired. Tension mounted as white loyalists grew jealous and angry with Black loyalists. Some even resorted to kidnapping and selling free Blacks back into slavery.

The tension led to the first full-blown race riot in North America in 1784. The Shelburne Riots started after a popular Black preacher, David George, had the nerve to baptize a white woman. A lynch mob attacked Pastor David, destroying his home, along with 20 other homes, on the first night. Over the next ten days, the mob continued burning and looting houses. It's unknown how many people were injured. Some may have been killed, although no deaths were recorded. By the end of the riot, the only Black people left in Shelburne besides a few free Blacks were slaves and servants.

Although the rampage was over, free Blacks in Nova Scotia still faced violence. They were treated the same, if not worse, than before. Many Black people left for the new settlement in Sierra Leone. Freetown was settled in 1787 by 400 former slaves sent from London.

Originally named Granville, the settlement was destroyed due to diseases and attacks by local natives. The British sent about 1,100 Black loyalists from Nova Scotia to reclaim the settlement, and Freetown was officially established in 1792.

Meanwhile, Black soldiers in America weren't getting quite what they were promised either. Connecticut passed the Gradual Emancipation Act in 1784, instead of completely outlawing slavery. The act only freed children born to enslaved mothers after the law was enacted. Anyone already enslaved was enslaved for life. Even children born after the law weren't free until the women turned 21, while men had to be 25. Rhode Island passed similar laws, which freed women at 18 and men at 21. Although Rhode Island enacted laws banning slavery in 1652, it wasn't enforced.

Many families in Rhode Island were heavily involved in the slave trade, including the Brown family the Ivy League school Brown University was named after. Colonial colleges were built by slaves and funded by the slave trade. The earliest schools included Harvard, Yale, Princeton, Dartmouth, William and Mary, Columbia University, Rutgers, and the University of Pennsylvania. Some were started on plantations.

By 1784, America's focus was on colonizing land to the west. North Carolina passed laws against importing slaves, but the debate was about legalizing slavery in new territories.

Thomas Jefferson is credited with creating the Land Ordinance of 1784. The plan included a clause to prohibit slavery in new territories after 1800. Congress rejected it, however.

Although Jefferson's plan supported abolishing slavery, he still felt Black people were inferior. He wrote about supporting freedom based on Negros being educated and assimilated into white society. Jefferson said women should be freed at 18 and men at 21. Later, he stated, no one should be freed until the age of 45 if a slaveholder had a return on investment. In a letter to Patrick Henry, Jefferson wrote Black people were mentally inferior to whites and incapable of producing a single poet. He routinely criticized and took shots at Phillis Wheatley because she was a Black woman who proved him wrong.

Although some states gradually passed laws to abolish slavery, New

York did not.

Instead, they passed a law requiring Negro and mulatto slaves to carry lanterns at night. They also prohibited them from fishing or riding horses in a "disorderly" fashion, and only allowed funerals for slaves during the daytime. If anyone violated the law, it resulted in a public flogging unless the owner paid a fine. Still, free Blacks created the New York African Society in 1784. A rich slave owner named John Jay also formed the New York Manumission Society. Jay still owned slaves and often debated about Negros getting rights after they were free. In 1785, he proposed a bill to free slaves in New York eventually, but it was rejected.

That year, Virginia passed legislation to classify biracial people as Negros. It was clear where biracial people stood. The law changed the definition of "mulatto" to anyone with at least a fourth or more Negro blood, or anyone with at least one Black grandparent, even if the others were white. When it was time for Virginia to free slaves who helped fight in the war, a bill was passed that extended rights only to free white inhabitants. As for Negros, the bill said, "No person henceforth shall be a slave except those already enslaved and their descendants." Essentially, the law didn't free anyone.

Instead, Virginia enacted stricter slave codes than before. Slaves were required to have a pass or a license to leave the plantation. Every Negro was forbidden from carrying arms or unlawfully assembling in groups of more than three. Each white person was deputized to enforce the code. If an enslaved person ran away, they could be apprehended by anyone white, and the owner had to reward them. If they couldn't find the owner, the slave was put in jail and could be hired out by the state. If no one claimed them after a year from the last advertisement in the lost slave section of the Virginia Gazette, they were sold.

Despite promises of freedom during the war, Virginia passed laws labeling Negros as property. If someone white lost their horses, cattle, or any property, including human beings, it had to be returned to the owner. "Wandering slaves" were put in jail for up to three months unless the owner came sooner. Many slaveholders let them go find jobs on their own if they paid a commission. But Virginia passed a law forbidding slaves from looking for work, even with permission. Anyone caught could be taken by the sheriff and sold to different owners. By this point, enslaved people were considered money. If someone owed a debt of more than $20, they were used as compensation.

Laws were passed to address European illegal immigrants still coming to Virginia under indentures as well. In most cases, as overseers, their contracts were not to exceed seven years, and their masters were required to provide for them. If they were injured or their owner failed to perform his duties, all contracts were void and they were discharged from service.

In the North, slavery was supposed to be ending gradually. The 14th colony, Vermont, banned selling and transporting Negros and mulattos out of the state. In Pennsylvania, while colonizers held the constitutional convention, prominent Black ministers Richard Allen and Absalom Jones founded the Free African Society of Philadelphia. During the 1787 convention led by George Washington, they discussed how to handle the Negro issue as well as how to deal with the white population. After the war, they not only feared slaves uprising, but also whites rebelling.

One uprising known as Shay's Rebellion started after white farmers expressed resentment against the wealthy and claimed they were being oppressed. Only white male landowners were allowed to vote, and many felt they were being taxed so much they'd lose their land and voting rights. Although Samuel Adams was a rebel himself 10 years earlier, he called for the execution of rebellious farmers.

At the time, America was still governed by the Articles of Confederation. Many felt the document was too weak to govern a nation and saw this as an opportunity to create something better. They wanted to form a stronger central government with more control over the states, which were basically seen as different countries. They devised a plan to form three branches of government and created the executive, legislative, and judicial branches. The goal was to separate and distribute the powers of the federal government. In the system of "checks and balances", the legislative branch makes the law, the judicial branch interprets the law, and the executive branch enforces the law.

They created the Constitution based on all men being created equal and entitled to certain inalienable rights. These hypocritical thugs, known as the "founding fathers," drafted this document of alleged equality while owning other human beings in the room, treating them like property. Although the original document didn't mention the word "slave," one clause in it was the three-fifths compromise. Southern states were bigger and had a larger population. Since there were more plantations in the South, there was a larger slave population as well. They argued slaves should be counted in the population, although they wouldn't have any representation.

Northern states disagreed, arguing slaves were property and shouldn't be counted any more than livestock. From the beginning, Southern states were ready to secede from the Union before it was officially formed. Instead, the North and South agreed on the three-fifths compromise, with three out of every five slaves being counted in the population. Another clause in the Constitution prohibited the government from abolishing the slave trade for at least 20 years.

After the Revolutionary War, many enslaved people in the South escaped. Also, the slave trade slowed down when the colonists stopped doing business with the British. The South wanted to replenish the slave population and imported countless captives over the next few years. While the Constitution didn't mention the word "slave," there was a clause that referred to runaway slaves. According to the Fugitives from Labor Clause, if a slave escaped to another state, even if that state prohibited slavery, they must be returned to the owner.

Some also argued the Fifth Amendment stopped the government from interfering in a person's right to own slaves because slaves were considered property. But it became a question of which states would forbid slavery and which ones would allow it. In 1787, Rhode Island and Delaware placed more restrictions on slave trading. North Carolina chose to raise taxes on slaves imported into the colony.

Ultimately, America adopted the Northwest Ordinance of 1787 to govern new territories in the Northwest. The ordinance forbade slavery in what became Ohio, Indiana, Illinois, Michigan, and Wisconsin. The Ohio River was the dividing line between free and slave states. Although it was outlawed in the new territories, residents were still required to return runaways. If a captive went to a free territory with the owner, they were still considered a slave.

The Constitution wasn't officially adopted until it was ratified by nine states in 1788. Although New York was one of the states that ratified it, they also adopted new slave codes. Even while importing enslaved people into New York was prohibited, illegal slave trading continued. New York declared anyone already enslaved as a slave for life.

After learning about the Constitution, free Negros in Boston petitioned for equal schools for free Black children. The African Free School was founded in New York that year.

Connecticut and Massachusetts continued to pass laws restricting the slave trade as well. Every slaver was required to register each child born enslaved. Pennsylvania amended the law by forbidding Negros from being removed from the state. Down South, former and current slaves officially founded the First African Baptist Church of Savannah, the first Black church in Georgia.

By 1789, it seemed certain parts of America were on pace to abolish slavery gradually.

In Delaware, slave trading across state lines was outlawed. For many, however, gradually ending slavery wasn't good enough. Although the Underground Railroad didn't reach its height until the 1850s with Harriet Tubman, it was founded in 1789. An ex-slave, Olaudah Equiano, also published his autobiography The Interesting Narrative of the Life of Olaudah Equiano in 1789. As one of the earliest Black writings published, it was a firsthand account highlighting an enslaved person's experience. Also, in Jamaica, the Drax Free School was founded, but enslaved children weren't allowed to attend.

Despite states passing laws for gradual emancipation, pro-slavery propaganda was still on the rise. Popular plays like The Benevolent Planters were published to promote slavery as a necessary institution. Eventually, America elected George Washington to be the first president. When Washington became president, he owned over 200 slaves. He wrote, the Quaker anti- slavery petitions were not only ill-judged but a great waste of time. Quaker apologist, though not a formal member, Benjamin Franklin died the next year.

America took its first Census in 1790. Black people made up 19 percent of the population, but only 9 percent of them were considered free. In Virginia, the slave population increased from 100,000 in 1756 to 200,000 in 1790. There were at least 292,627 slaves on record in Virginia, the most of any colony. By comparison, New Hampshire had a total of 157 slaves. With a total population of around 4 million, there were only 59,557 free Blacks compared to 697,624 enslaved people. Most of the free population lived near the Chesapeake area. Many free and enslaved Blacks got caught up in The Second Great Awakening after 1790. The number of documented Black Christians increased by about 12,000.

As America was taking shape, DC (The District of Columbia) was chosen as the nation's capital. Despite a European taking credit, it was Benjamin Banneker who originally designed DC. When the lead designer quit the project and took the plans with him, Benjamin recreated the design in two days. Like many Black inventors, he still doesn't get credit for much of his work.

Free Blacks were forced to create their own organizations, such as the Brown Fellowship Society in Charleston, S.C.. Unlike the church, the Brown Fellowship Society was a self-help organization that banned religious discussions. However, membership was limited to biracial people, and they referred to themselves as brown instead of Black. The Brown Fellowship Society refused to get involved in slavery because they didn't want to upset the white community. Some members could pass for white and owned slaves themselves.

But Congress was in the middle of making white nationalism official in America. The Naturalization Act of 1790 was the first immigration law passed in America. Citizenship was only granted to "free white persons of good character." Now officially a white nation, many states adopted laws to force free Negros to leave within a certain time or face punishment.

Charles Pinckney was a slave owner who helped write the Constitution and signed it. Pinckney said at the time the document was drafted, he knew perfectly there was no such thing as a Negro citizen, nor could he conceive it ever possibly existing.

Regardless of which side of the war Black people fought on, it resulted in empty promises. They still faced the same treatment and discrimination despite the cries of "give me liberty or give me death." African Americans found out the hard way that didn't apply to them. Congress advocated expanding slavery into the Southwest. The first promise of freedom persuaded them to join the fight, but there were already plenty of reasons not to trust the words of Europeans. This wasn't the first time they didn't keep their word, nor would it be the last.

CHAPTER 6.
THE FUGITIVE ACTS: A REVOLUTION IN HAITI

Arguably, slavery in the Caribbean was much worse, though demographics were considerably different. In the West Indies, seven-eighths of the population were Black, yet only 3% were free. By 1790, Haiti was under French rule and became the wealthiest colony in the "new world," mostly because of sugar. Rumors of how sugar plantation owners treated slaves were infamous globally. Owners often threatened to send rebellious slaves there to be tamed.

After the French Revolution began, the people of Saint-Domingue were even more inspired to fight back. If French colonists fought against rising taxes, they could fight for their freedom. In Paris, freeborn Blacks enjoyed the same rights as whites. But in Saint-Domingue, free Blacks were treated as bad as slaves. Some free Negros tried to be accepted by the French, even dressing, walking, and talking like them. A few free Blacks owned slaves as well, although the law didn't protect their right to own any kind of property. No matter what they did, they were never respected. Still, some Negros chose to fight with white slave owners during rebellions.

Half of the free Black population were of mixed race. Unlike the English, the French claimed the children they had with enslaved women, using it to their advantage. People of mixed race owned about 10 percent of the slaves in Haiti, some becoming as rich as European owners. Since Negros heavily outnumbered Europeans, biracial people were used to keep the slave population in check. They maintained control by reinforcing colorist concepts. The lighter your skin, the more benefits you enjoyed. The darker your skin, the worse you were treated.

The French divided the population to keep them from uniting and rising up. Still, many slaves escaped captivity and organized. Led by an ex-slave, Toussaint Louverture, the maroons, or runaway slaves, met in swampy areas so they wouldn't be discovered. During the ceremony at the Bois Caiman, the maroons planned their attack and performed a Vodou ritual to prepare. Despite stereotypes, Vodou isn't negative or spooky; it's an ancient spiritual practice of being one with nature. In this case, they used Vodou to conjure the spirit of Ogun, the energy of a powerful warrior. Not long after the ceremony, the revolution was underway.

They gained momentum as plantations burned to the ground, and soon, more people joined. The uprising had such an impact, Paris issued a decree granting free Negros and mulattos equal citizenship. However, many whites objected to it, adding fuel to the fire. Within a few weeks, about 100,000 slaves joined the rebellion. Around 900 plantations, crops, fields, and buildings were burned to the ground. Close to 4,000 whites were killed. A few months after Paris's decree, they rescinded the offer for Black citizenship. France sent troops and officials to restore order, but Port-au-Prince was burned to the ground.

As the fighting continued, a leader in the rebellion, Dutty Boukman, was captured. They called him Boukman because he could read and often tried to teach others. As a priest, he led the ceremony at the Bois Caiman. Once he was captured, they decapitated him and put his head on a spike for all to see. But instead of being intimidated, it only inspired them to fight harder.

The revolution in 1791 wasn't the beginning, but not all resistance was obvious. Slaves also used their knowledge of nature to poison their captors whenever possible. Years before the revolution, a maroon named Francois Makandal taught slaves how to poison their owners and overseers discretely. With extensive knowledge of nature, Francois planned to remove whites from power by any means necessary. However, he was captured in 1758 and sentenced to burn at the stake.

As word of Francois Makandal's plan spread, it had such an effect on America, Georgia passed a law forbidding teaching slaves about plants and anything potentially poisonous.

Although there was friction from the start, Europeans were unprepared for what was about to happen.

Using European feuds over greed to their advantage, the rebellion gained momentum. France offered amnesty to the maroons if they stopped fighting and peacefully submitted to slavery. When they refused, the governor, Philibert de Blanchelande, beheaded hundreds of men, women, and children, including the elderly, and ordered their bodies to be chopped to pieces. The French captured about 3,000 maroons and forced them back into slavery. But they were unable to retake the land.

Before the monarchy system in France was abolished in 1792, the last king, Louis XVI, reinstated the decree to grant free Blacks and biracial people equal rights. But it didn't outlaw slavery. Since European nations declared war on each other, the Haitians allied with the British to push the French out. The streets were a battlefield.

France became desperate, begging Black soldiers to fight with them. Using similar tactics as the Revolutionary War, France offered freedom and full citizenship to any Black person who helped defend the colony. However, France refused to meet the demands of the maroons. Most colonists were upset France even considered making Negros an offer. By 1792, the enslaved population took over at least a third of the island.

Spain also joined the war against France in 1793. Not only were they fighting over the most lucrative colony in the "new world," Spain feared the rebellion would inspire slaves in the Dominican Republic to do the same. Toussaint Louverture did what he could to help the French.

He even offered aid to General Laveaux. Toussaint was willing to give 5,000 to 6,000 troops for freedom and equal rights, but the French refused the offer. Although neither side officially offered freedom, Haitians felt the conditions with the Spanish were less harsh. With help from the British and Spanish, soon there were only 3,500 French troops left in Haiti.

France was forced to give in to the demands of the Haitians. They issued a new decree, offering freedom to any slave, their wife, and their children if they helped France keep the colony. Toussaint gained control of the entire northern part of the island after becoming allies with the Spanish. In desperation, the French National Assembly abolished slavery in all its colonies, including Haiti. One text written by a European predicted the rise of a Black leader. Known as the "Black Spartacus," Toussaint wrote a letter to the people promising them freedom if they made him a leader. Europeans always had a fear of a Black messiah or leader rising up. But there wasn't just one leader; revolution is an energy. Black unity is the Black messiah.

By organizing enough people and properly training them in the art of guerrilla warfare, Toussaint ended slavery in Haiti by 1795. Before the fighting began, he sent his former owners off the island so they wouldn't be killed. He saw himself as French and wanted to be accepted by them. Toussaint no longer supported Spain and encouraged others to fight with France.

Eventually, Spain and France officially agreed to end the war in 1795. The Peace of Basel treaty split Hispaniola into two separate colonies. Spain controlled the Dominican Republic, and France controlled Haiti. News of what happened in Haiti quickly spread to both slaves and owners around the world.

In America, Vermont was admitted into the Union in 1791, supposedly as a free state.

The law stated, no person is bound by law to serve or be enslaved by another after the age of 21 for men and 18 for women. Although the Bill of Rights had just been ratified, each state was still considered its own nation, governed by its own laws. After the nation's capital was moved to DC, a French American, Pierre Charles L'Enfant, used slaves to build The White House and capitol building.

Prior to DC becoming the nation's capital, George Washington spent much of his time as president in Pennsylvania. Since Pennsylvania was a free state, Washington was forced to send his slaves back to Virginia to avoid losing his "property." A Pennsylvania law allowed enslaved people to make a claim for freedom after being in the state for at least six months.

Regardless of what Washington said about the institution of slavery, he had no problem with slave trading himself. As president, he sent a slave named Jack to the West Indies to be disposed of, as he did with many rebellious or runaway slaves. It's said that Washington once threatened to send a 15-year-old boy to the West Indies like he did Jack the wagon driver if he didn't straighten up.

Still, America chose to reelect George Washington in 1792. John Adams was appointed as vice president. That year, Kentucky split from Virginia and was admitted into the Union as a slave state. After the war was over, Washington planned to disarm Negros once again. Congress passed the Militia Acts of 1792 to ban Black men from serving in the army. After America depended on Black soldiers to defend the colonies, it was clear the Second Amendment and the Constitution itself didn't apply to Negros. Instead, the Buttonwood Agreement was signed, officially establishing the New York Stock Exchange. The stock exchange was set up a block away from the slave market. The agreement covered all transactions dealing with the slave trade, from insuring slaves to human trafficking.

As a slave state, Delaware decided to exclude free Blacks from voting. As bad as things were, after 1793, it got much worse. Before Eli Whitney received a patent for the cotton gin, sugar and tobacco were the main source of income for America. After the cotton gin, the demand for cotton exploded, leading to a greater demand for slaves. The only way to keep up with the demand was to work slaves much harder. They were forced to pick cotton from before sunrise to after sunset while being treated worse than before. The number of slaves increased from thousands to millions. One out of every three Black people was enslaved.

Once America learned how to mass-produce cotton, they used slaves to build their wealth and empire. The beatings and torture slaves endured were taken to another level. They were punished for not picking enough cotton for the day. By law, owners were required to provide for slaves, but after working all day, they barely had any food. They received one pair of cheap shoes per year, if they were lucky. Once they wore out, they had to go without them, regardless of the weather. If an enslaved person refused to work or didn't work hard enough, they threatened to whip them, to sell their family, or to castrate them.

One of George Washington's captives, Charlotte, often worked in the house. One day, she refused to do what an overseer told her. It could've been anything, including rape, but the overseer whipped her for not complying. Charlotte hadn't been whipped in 14 years. She thought she was different from the other slaves and accepted by Washington. Of course, Washington and his wife sided with the overseer. They gave him the authority to whip Charlotte anytime he wanted.

Some slaves learned the hard way, no matter how much they obeyed, they were only seen as property. When the yellow fever epidemic broke out in Philadelphia, many colonists died. The slaves with the "we sick, boss" mentality were infected and died after caring for their owners.

Despite America's promise of freedom after the war, George Washington passed the Fugitive Slave Act of 1793. This act changed the meaning of being a free Negro. No Black person was safe. This was the first Fugitive Slave Law that applied to every state under the Constitution, although some states already had laws in place. The Fugitive Slave Act allowed owners and random white citizens to capture any Negro they suspected of being a runaway slave, including in free states. Once captured, they faced a judge. Whether they were free or a runaway, the judge usually gave their kidnapper legal custody of them. Kidnapping and selling people became a way for some whites to earn money.

The free Black population, especially children, faced a constant threat of being kidnapped and sold into slavery. The number of people kidnapped skyrocketed, similar to the depiction in the movie 12 Years a Slave. Whites kidnapped so many free Blacks, a law was passed to prevent free Black children from being taken and sold into slavery. However, the law was rarely enforced. Countless free Black men, women, and children were taken from their homes and found themselves in chains. If anyone tried to help a slave or allowed them to take refuge, they were punished with anything from a fine up to death.

Essentially, slavery was nationalized in America. Every Negro, no matter where they were, fit the description and was at risk every time they left home. After the cotton gin was created, the price of slaves increased along with demand. Virginia passed laws forbidding free Negros from even entering the state. Every Black person in Virginia was assumed to be a slave.

The kidnapping trade extended beyond American borders as well. A Black woman named Chloe Cooley was abducted from Canada and sold into slavery in America. After Chloe was taken, Canada passed laws to limit slavery near Ontario. However, no one was freed.

Twelve of the twenty-five Canadian government officials and their family members owned slaves. Canada's first and only anti-slavery legislation declared any children born to an enslaved woman wouldn't be freed until age 25, but anyone already enslaved would be a slave for life. Although the act somewhat limited importing and exporting slaves, slave trading continued as usual within their borders. Many slave catchers also continued to pursue runaway slaves into Canada.

America went from producing 140,000 pounds of cotton in 1791 to 35 million pounds by 1800. But as news of the revolution in Haiti spread, America limited captives from being imported. Despite an increase in demand, even states like Georgia prohibited slaves from being imported in 1798. The law wasn't enforced because of the large number of plantations in Georgia. The slave population rose from 30,000 in 1790 to 60,000 in 1800. By 1810, there were over 105,000 slaves in Georgia alone.

America's greed outweighed its fear and guilt. In 1794, Congress passed a law forbidding enslaved people from being exported to any foreign place to benefit another nation. An additional law prohibited whites from equipping ships to transport slaves out of America. Still, neither law stopped or limited people from taking slaves in and out of America.

In the face of worsening conditions, people like Richard Allen continued the struggle for Black liberation. After buying his own freedom, Richard founded the Bethel A.M.E church in Philadelphia in 1794. During The Second Great Awakening, Black people converted to Christianity in large numbers. In many cases, it was beaten into them. White churches fully practiced white supremacy, so Black people created their own churches. In New York, Black Christians built the Mother African Methodist Episcopal Zion Church for a Black congregation, although a few whites attended.

Influenced by the events in Haiti, more violent forms of resistance persisted. The Spanish still controlled Louisiana in 1795. Some of the enslaved population planned a revolt to take their freedom. Before the Pointe Coupee Conspiracy could take place, they were betrayed by two Tunica Indian women. They overheard the plans to revolt and told authorities. They claimed slaves were planning to kill all white people. The Indian women said they'd fear for their lives if the uprising was successful.

In response, Spanish authorities sent patrols to arrest any Black person at a plantation where they didn't belong. The governor ordered the patrols to raid slave quarters from Louisiana to West Florida. They confiscated anything that could be used as a weapon and arrested anyone they considered a stranger. Within a few months, they executed at least 23 people and placed their heads on spikes along the Mississippi River to send a message. One of the alleged leaders, a free man named Antonio Cofi Mina, was deported to Havana.

The Dutch in Curacao had to deal with their own revolt. Led by Tula Rigaud, 40 or 50 slaves told their owner they were no longer slaves. They said if he didn't like it to go complain to the lieutenant governor. They walked off the plantation before freeing 22 others. They went from plantation to plantation, freeing anyone who wanted to join them. Simultaneously, Louis Mercier, who was enslaved by the French, led another group of freed slaves. Louis and his group took ten mulatto soldiers as prisoners. When Tula and Louis met up in Saint Kruis, many slavers fled the city.

Tula and Louis were aware of the Haitian Revolution. They felt since the Netherlands was captured by the French, they were entitled to freedom as well. Tula made three demands. First, they demanded to end the collective punishment of Negros. Their second demand was to end labor on Sundays. The final demand was for freedom to buy food, clothes, and to conduct business with people other than their enslaver.

The Dutch tried to negotiate twice, but these warriors wouldn't accept anything less than freedom. After negotiations failed, a Dutch Captain, Baron Van Westerholt, issued an order to kill any slave caught with a weapon. Twenty-two freedom fighters were killed, but the rest managed to escape. The rebels used guerrilla warfare tactics to fight back. They poisoned wells and stole their food. At the height of the rebellion, Tula was able to unite close to 1,000 warriors.

The rebellion lasted a few months until Tula was betrayed by a slave who was captured. He was publicly tortured to death to send others a message. Louis Mercier, along with two other leaders, Karpata and Pedro Wakao, were also executed. Many enslaved people were massacred by the Dutch if they were suspected of being involved, whether they were or not. Still, no matter how severe the punishment, the fight for freedom persisted.

Before the Haitian Revolution, there was Tacky's War in Jamaica in 1760. Tacky (Takyi) was kidnapped from Ghana along with an Asante queen named Nanny (Nana). They planned to take Jamaica from the British and make it a Black nation. After taking over their plantation, they broke into a gun store and killed the owner. They stole 40 guns and 4 barrels of gunpowder.

Eventually, hundreds of people joined them. However, a slave warned British authorities. Britain had already signed treaties with a group of maroons. In exchange for freedom, the maroons agreed to be the slave patrol. They were often sent in to stop revolts or catch runaway slaves, although they were former slaves. Black people have always been used to do what Europeans couldn't, including stopping uprisings and Black unity. By the time the revolt was over, 60 white people were killed. Over 400 Black people died as well. Tacky was decapitated, and his head was put on a spike in the middle of town. The British set out to punish anyone they suspected was involved. Still, conflicts continued for months.

In Kingston, an Asante woman named Cubah Cornwallis was elected to be queen. The people gave her the title of "Queen of Kingston." When British authorities found out, they tried to send her off the island. Cubah managed to escape and continued fighting in western Jamaica until she was captured and executed.

By this point, white fear and guilt had caused them to blame and execute Black people for everything. In Albany, NY, a fire destroyed 26 homes, stores, and buildings in 1793. Whites immediately blamed Negros, and they were rounded up and interrogated randomly. Every slave became subject to stricter laws and earlier curfews. They eventually blamed the fire on three enslaved children—two young Black girls, Dinah who was 14, and Bet who was 12—were lynched. A month later, a 16-year-old boy named Pompey was arrested and hung. They didn't have any evidence, nor did they know what caused the fire. They forced these children into false confessions, something America has a long history of.

When George Washington's slaves tried to escape, he published ads for their return but asked they not be shown north of Virginia. In Georgetown in 1795, an ordinance outlawed five or more slaves from congregating. If anyone was caught, they'd received 39 lashes and their owner was fined $3. Although there was never an Irish slave in America, the ordinance affected indentured servants as well.

Free or enslaved, Black people realized to be free, they'd have to take it into their own hands. America offered freedom when they needed Black people to join the fight, then passed laws jeopardizing even those who were already free. Yet, it was seeing Europeans refuse to be oppressed over taxes they owed that helped inspire not only the Haitian Revolution but many others.

CHAPTER 7.
THE CASTE SYSTEM: A
STRUGGLE FOR POWER

Historically, mulattos, Black people, and white supremacy have had a complicated relationship. In many cases, biracial people ended up on the extreme of either side. In a system that awards more privileges the lighter your skin is, many rejected their Black side for making them feel inferior, especially if they passed for white. But just as many embraced their Blackness, fighting, even dying for Black liberation. Many biracial people feel they've never been accepted by either side. But in the system of white supremacy, they're seen as just another Negro.

By 1796, Toussaint and the Haitian warriors took control of the island. However, the mulatto class, many of whom were slave owners before the revolution, felt their slaves should be returned. In Haiti, more so than other places, biracial people saw themselves in a higher class than darker-skinned Haitians. Since they had white blood, slave owners let mulattos run their plantations. Many felt superior and abused their newly acquired authority over darker-skinned Haitians. Jean-Louis Villatte, a biracial commander, felt he deserved to take leadership from Toussaint.

Villatte was known to be prejudiced toward darker-skinned people. Feeling threatened by new policies, he led a group of biracial people to capture General Laveaux. Villatte planned on charging him with tyranny after addressing the prejudiced behavior darker-skinned Haitians faced.

Laveaux was thrown in prison until Toussaint ordered his release. Afterward, Laveaux named Toussaint lieutenant governor and said he wouldn't make any decisions without consulting him first. Laveaux eventually left the island and became a representative for Toussaint in France. As the last Spanish troops withdrew from Hispaniola, Toussaint was appointed commander and chief of the army. Not only were the Spanish expelled from Haiti, they were also losing ground in America.

After Pinckney's Treaty was signed, America gained access to more land in Florida and could engage in trading along the Mississippi River without being taxed by the Spanish.

With America's territory expanding, Tennessee was admitted into the Union as a slave state in 1796. Technically, free Black men could vote, but the law limited voting rights to males 21 and up who had at least 200 acres of land. Conversely, in New York, the first state-sponsored school for free Black children was created in 1797. Still, New York continued to procrastinate on abolishing slavery. Instead, more gradual emancipation legislation was passed. The law stated, "any children born to enslaved women after July 4, 1799, will be considered free legally." In reality, they were still enslaved until the age of 28 for men and 25 for women.

Anyone born prior to that date was labeled an indentured servant instead of a slave, but they remained in bondage for life. Since the great Sojourner Truth was born in New York in 1797, by law, she was condemned to be a slave for life, despite being called an "indentured servant." Sojourner refused to be kept in bondage and eventually escaped, going on to help many others.

Nonetheless, for the first time, free Blacks in Philadelphia, as a collective, petitioned Congress to end the institution of slavery. Four free Black men who were kidnapped and sold into slavery inspired their protest. Jacob and Jupiter Nicholson, Joe Albert, and Turner Pritchett earned their freedom by fighting in the Revolutionary War, although their families were still enslaved in North Carolina. In a city with so many "righteous abolitionists," these four men were held against their will under the Fugitive Slave Act. Despite having proof and witnesses, Congress voted against even receiving the petition with a vote of fifty to thirty-three.

After John Adams was elected the second president in 1797, Spain began leaving the territory, which later became Mississippi. Congress made sure the new area, which included parts of Alabama, was a slave state under the Northwest Ordinance of 1787. With so many cotton fields in Mississippi and a growing demand after the cotton gin was invented, a mass migration increased the population from close to 10,000 to 30,000 by 1798, and around 200,000 by 1817.

Likewise, the slave population in Mississippi increased from about 4,000 in 1798 to 70,000 in 1817. To replace the slave population in Georgia, many slaves were imported directly from Africa between 1794-1798. Seventy-eight percent of the slaves brought into Savannah, GA, alone were imported from Africa. After Georgia drafted its state Constitution, they added a statute to prevent slaves from being imported into the state.

Meanwhile, in Boston, MA, the first state-sponsored school for free Black children was established in 1798. Nonetheless, America was understanding that kids born into slavery were a lot easier to control than those who had known freedom. People born into slavery could be indoctrinated and were more likely to accept bondage. Thanks to the Haitian Revolution, colonies became increasingly cautious about importing slaves into their state.

As president, John Adams recognized Saint-Domingue's government and Toussaint as its leader. But Toussaint's recognition angered and scared Thomas Jefferson, who believed the energy of revolution would spread throughout the states and cause Negros in America to do the same.

Most of the land in Saint-Domingue under English control had been taken by Toussaint by 1798. After forcing their surrender, Toussaint granted amnesty to French citizens who chose not to fight with the British, along with the Black soldiers in their army. Although Toussaint saw himself as a French citizen and general, French authorities wanted to make sure Negros stayed in their place. In fear of Toussaint and his army's power, French officials like Theodore Hedouville were sent to enforce French law.

Hedouville attempted to use divide-and-conquer techniques to disband Toussaint's army. Andre Rigaud, leader of a mixed-race army, had respect for Toussaint but still believed in a race-based caste system. Believing biracial people were superior created rifts people like Hedouville tried to exploit. Still, his efforts to cause division failed, and Jean-Jacques Dessalines was sent to arrest him. Toussaint was off signing a secret non-aggression treaty with England and America. Although the treaty reopened trade for Haiti, animosity between darker- skinned Haitians and those of mixed-race exploded into a civil war between Toussaint and

Rigaud in 1799.

America, on the other hand, dealt with biracial people much differently. Virginia passed a law to ban white mothers with mulatto children from the colony completely. George Washington died in Virginia that year. In his will, he said his slaves were to be freed after his wife died, but half of them remained enslaved for decades. His wife, Martha, only freed some of them because she believed they were poisoning her. The rest were divided among her children, despite Washington's promise of freedom.

For many, the only way to get freedom was to emancipate themselves. At the start of the 19th century, an enslaved man in Richmond, VA, Gabriel Prosser, planned a revolt later known as Gabriel's Rebellion. Gabriel was born in 1776, a time when the energy of revolution was in the air. Despite laws against educating slaves, Gabriel still learned how to read and write. After becoming a blacksmith, his job allowed him to move around the city more than others, and he met many people. His enslaver, Thomas Prosser, owned a huge tobacco farm called The Brookfield Plantation. He often leased out Gabriel to make a profit, but it gave Gabriel a chance to congregate with slaves from other plantations.

One day, Gabriel, his brother, and a friend were caught stealing a pig. Slaves worked from sunup to sundown, but barely had enough food to survive. Out of hunger, sometimes slaves were forced to steal just to eat. Although it was out of desperation, Europeans used the situation to create the myth that Black people were naturally prone to stealing. When Prosser's neighbor confronted Gabriel and the others about the pig, Gabriel was tired of bowing down, keeping his eyes to the ground. He refused to tap dance or beg for forgiveness, and the confrontation turned into a scuffle.

During the altercation, Gabriel bit a piece of the neighbor's ear off. Now, instead of being arrested for stealing a pig, he was charged with harming a white male, a federal offense. Although he was supposed to be hung, Gabriel was granted a benefit of clergy, allowing him to recite a Bible verse to avoid execution. He was still whipped, publicly humiliated, and branded to show he was a felon. He spent a month in prison before being sent back to the Brookfield plantation.

After meeting a slave named Jack Ditcher, they began meeting with other like-minded people on Sundays. Gathering at Young Spring, now Bryan Park, they organized a plan to take their freedom. One day, after a funeral, Gabriel stood up and asked for help with his plan to kill every white slave owner and overseer. They planned to split into three groups. The first group was supposed to start a fire in the warehouse district, now Rocketts Landing, to distract the militia. The second group was supposed to go to the armory, where they had someone to let them in. Once armed, they were supposed to meet the third group coming from Petersburg at the capitol to take Governor James Monroe hostage. They only wanted to negotiate for freedom and economic opportunities.

As a blacksmith, Gabriel made weapons. Using Patrick Henry's quote, they created a flag saying "death or liberty" to show their mindset. The night they planned to meet, a severe thunderstorm stopped most from showing up. Gabriel, his wife, Nanny, and Jack Ditcher still wanted to proceed. But without enough people to execute the plan, they were forced to postpone until the next day. It's said that Gabriel organized close to 1,000 people, but before they could meet the next day, authorities were informed.

Two slaves, Pharaoh and Tom, felt "close" with their master, so they told him about Gabriel's plan. When James Madison got word, he sent the militia around Richmond to arrest anyone they suspected was involved. Gabriel was forced to flee. He made it to the James River and found someone willing to take him to Norfolk. However, two slaves named Ishim and Billy recognized Gabriel. They tried to tell the ship's captain who he was, but the captain helped him anyway. When they arrived in Norfolk, Ishim and Billy notified white authorities, and both Gabriel and the captain were arrested.

They held Gabriel's trial on October 6, 1800. They tried to get him to explain the plan and tell on other people involved. Being the warrior Gabriel was, he didn't say a word. During sentencing, he requested to be executed alongside everyone else. They executed Gabriel on the same day as everyone else, but in a different location. Disrespecting his wishes, Gabriel was hung alone. They forced other slaves to watch the lynching to send a message, but Gabriel went out like a soldier. He refused to give them the satisfaction of seeing him struggle or plead for mercy. Gabriel was a warrior until the end.

The two slaves who turned him in were only given a $50 reward, not even enough to buy their freedom. Thomas Prosser, on the other hand, was compensated with $500 for his death because he was Gabriel's owner. At least 25 others were executed after the attempted rebellion.

Virginia quickly changed the law to forbid owners from freeing slaves. They wanted to bury the memory of Gabriel as fast as possible so no one else would have any ideas about uprising. Any free Negros still in the state after a certain time were subject to becoming enslaved. It also became illegal for slaves to learn how to read, write, or to be educated at all. All Negros, free or enslaved, were forbidden from gathering in groups or arming themselves.

In 1800, the second U.S. Census was taken. America had a population of 5.3 million, including 1 million Black people, but 900,000 were enslaved. America elected Thomas Jefferson, another slave owner, to be the third president. Many believed during the election, John Adams was the one who exposed Jefferson's sick relationship with Sally Hemings. Older white males sexually abusing young Black and biracial girls was common. Women who they considered the most beautiful stayed in the "big house" so they could rape them at any time.

White women were often jealous of Black women and girls because their husbands preferred enslaved women to them. They usually treated Black women worst of all, brutalizing them more than anyone.

After Jefferson became president, Congress passed a law restricting Americans from exporting slaves out of the country. Congress also passed legislation in support of sending free Negros to Africa. However, they'd still be under American law and subject to taxes. Many freedmen rejected the legislation, knowing it wasn't true freedom.

Back in Haiti, Jean-Jacques Dessalines defeated Rigaud by 1800, with a little help from America. Rigaud was exiled to France, giving Toussaint and his army uncontested control of Saint-Domingue. After Spain conceded the rest of their territory, Toussaint finally gained control over the entire island. Once in power, he created new policies to reenforce the traditional plantation system. He planned to import more Africans to Haiti, hoping to increase the workforce. Toussaint wanted to fix the economy by selling goods to France, but many felt this was his way of reimposing slavery. Curious about the extent of Toussaint's power, Napoleon Bonaparte sent a commission to investigate and ultimately reinstate slavery in the colony.

Toussaint formed an assembly to write a new Constitution banning slavery in all of Hispaniola forever. Haiti's Constitution eliminated the differences in race and color, declaring, "All people shall be admitted based on merit." Anyone born on the island was considered a free and equal French citizen. However, Catholicism became Hispaniola's official religion, and the Constitution banned Vodou. On top of that, many workers resented it for codifying mandatory labor. They also begrudged Toussaint's desire to be accepted by the French. Although the Constitution wasn't a formal declaration of independence, it still held more power than French laws. Yet, Toussaint called Hispaniola a French island for the benefit of the French.

Toussaint simply wanted Saint-Domingue to be equal with France, but Bonaparte saw it as a threat and rejected it. Thomas Jefferson agreed with Bonaparte and pledged to support France's agenda. Therefore, America no longer recognized Saint-Domingue as a nation, and Bonaparte planned to regain control of the island to reenforce the Code Noir. Bonaparte sent his brother-in-law, General Victor Leclerc, to capture Toussaint and other leaders of the revolution. Many biracial slave owners welcomed Leclerc's arrival until they realized he viewed them no differently. Like Bonaparte, Leclerc knew the power of Black people and said their progress around the world needed to be stopped.

Since Toussaint remained loyal to the French, the Black and mixed-race population united to rebel against him. They felt as if they fought for freedom just to continue working for Europeans under Toussaint. For many, their goal was to kill every one of their oppressors.

Before Toussaint could stop the rebellion, about 250 whites and nearly 1,000 rebels were killed. Not only did he lose support from those of mixed-race, he was also losing support from his original followers.

Within a year, France sent 20,000 troops, known as the elite of the French army, to retake the island. With a corrupt general like Rochambeau in charge, the French created a specific three-stage plan. First, Rochambeau tried to convince the people that France had peaceful intentions and was only there to protect them. It lasted for about 15 to 20 days, while troops took the land, setting up bases to take control of major ports and cities. The second stage was to wage war on rebel armies when their guard was down and to take out their generals and leaders.

Bonaparte said, "Don't leave any Negros with a rank of captain or higher alive." The last stage was to disarm every Negro and mixed-race person and force them back on plantations by any means—even if it meant killing everybody and replacing them with Africans.

When the French army arrived in Haiti, Toussaint warned everyone they intended to reinstate slavery. The Haitians' plan was to burn all the coastal towns and retreat deep into the island where Europeans were afraid to go. They attacked sparingly when the French were off guard, using guerilla warfare tactics. Within three weeks, 500 French soldiers died and 1,000 more were wounded. Leclerc requested another 6,000 troops, plus an additional 2,000 troops per month for reinforcements. Yet, they still didn't stand a chance.

Bonaparte sent 408 ships carrying 80,000 troops between 1802-1803. But in the battle of Crete-a-Pierrot, it was the French that suffered major losses. Outnumbered 12,000 to 1,500, Dessalines and the Haitian warriors defeated an army ten times the size of theirs. With thousands of French soldiers dead and a third of their army wounded, Leclerc requested another 25,000 troops. Thirty to fifty French soldiers were dying in the hospital per day—not only from the war—but also from diseases like yellow fever.

Realizing they didn't have the power to carry out their plan, Bonaparte and Leclerc were forced to negotiate with Toussaint. Using Toussaint's desire to be accepted by the French against him, they offered for him to keep his military rank and retire anywhere he chose if he surrendered. Toussaint agreed, feeling as if he couldn't take any more losses. Dessalines, however, already understood not to trust the French and had no desire to be accepted by them. His only goal was freedom, and he took over the revolution.

Many tried to tell Toussaint not to trust the French. Sure enough, when he met with Bonaparte, he was betrayed. Once Bonaparte captured

Toussaint, they tried to force him to give up other leaders, but he refused. He shipped Toussaint to France, where he was held prisoner until he died the next year. With Toussaint out of the way, Bonaparte gained temporary control of the island. First, he issued a decree reinstating slavery in Martinique, Tobago, and Saint Lucie. Bonaparte insisted slavery wouldn't be reenforced in Guadeloupe or Saint-Domingue, but Dessalines and the Haitians knew better than to trust Europeans.

America took slavery up another notch as well. After Congress moved from Philadelphia to DC in 1801, Virginia's slave codes were introduced in DC and Maryland. The federal slave code established in DC included a law to prohibit importing slaves into the state to be sold. New York passed the same law, although owners could still bring their slaves into the state with them.

Some free states allowed slaves to petition for freedom if they stayed in the colony for an extended period. In the case, Sylvia v. Coryell, a Black woman successfully sued for her freedom. She was enslaved in Virginia, but when she was ten, her enslaver sent her to New Jersey to take care of his mother. After three years, she was sent back to Virginia, still considered a slave. When Sylvia got older, she realized she had a case to sue for her freedom.

She argued, since she had been in New Jersey for three years, she was entitled to freedom in the state. The courts agreed and ruled in her favor. Sylvia's former enslaver was forced to release her. Many free states had similar laws. When Ohio's state Constitution was drafted, it included clauses to abolish slavery. Still, with the Fugitive Slave Law in effect, free Black people weren't safe, even in free states. In colonies like Mississippi, a bill that would've prohibited slaves from being imported was rejected. Many states were terrified of the rebellious Negro, but greed outweighed fear in states with the most plantations. For the oppressed, it was freedom that needed to outweigh fear.

CHAPTER 8.
1804: THE 2ND WAR FOR INDEPENDENCE

Gunpowder wasn't the only thing that helped Europeans conquer land. Deception is another deadly tool in their arsenal. Remember, unlike Toussaint, Dessalines didn't trust the French and had no desire to be accepted by them. Dessalines's only goal was freedom, and he understood Europeans rarely kept their word. The people of Haiti saw Bonaparte's mission to reinstate slavery, regardless of what he said. With no other choice, Black and biracial people put aside their differences to form a new militia.

They attempted to force the French off the island. Thousands of Haitian troops used guerrilla warfare to attack the French. Once word reached Haiti that slavery was restored in Guadeloupe, the people were inspired to unite and fight harder, thinking they might be next. Black and mixed-race soldiers went to Haiti to join the army. Many French soldiers died from yellow fever and mutinies that broke out all over the island, and slave owners were killed.

An all-Black militia in Saint-Louis-du-Sud joined the rebellion, quickly taking control of the city. In retaliation, French soldiers killed every Black and mixed-race person they saw, whether they were involved or not. They planned to hunt down every Haitian soldier, but thousands joined the fight. They attacked cities and took over plantations. In a letter to Bonaparte, Leclerc said he believed the only way they'd accomplish their goals was to just kill everyone and import slaves from Africa to start over. Bonaparte agreed, but Leclerc died of yellow fever before he acted.

Before Leclerc died, he recommended General Rochambeau to take his place. Leclerc called Rochambeau a person of integrity and a good military man. Most importantly, he hated Negros and biracial people just as much. Even other Europeans saw Rochambeau as brutal.

There's a story of Rochambeau throwing a party for the wives of biracial soldiers who fought with the British. He offered them gifts to show his gratitude, but when they opened the boxes, they saw their husband's severed heads.

As soon as Rochambeau took command, he requested 35,000 troops to commit genocide. He also imported attack dogs from Cuba. They were bred to hunt Negros, and only ate the flesh of Black people. Even when Haitian troops surrendered, Rochambeau had men and women burned alive. Many were tortured, then executed by being set on fire, drowned, and even boiled alive. Rochambeau even killed Black soldiers on his side with Haitian prisoners by burning sulfur in the holds of ships.

Still, the people of Haiti were determined to take their freedom and were more united than ever. Even average citizens got involved by using guerrilla warfare to decimate French troops. Also plagued with diseases, the French were running out of troops, money, and supplies. They tried to make one last stand at Grand'Anse but failed. Everything that Rochambeau did, Dessalines responded in kind. For every 500 Haitians that were killed, 500 French soldiers were hung.

Many say the Haitians tried to kill every white person on the island, but that wasn't the case. They only attacked their French oppressors, slave owners, and those on their side. Other whites who sided with the Haitians, like the Polish and Germans, could stay. They were even classified as Black.

Eventually, Dessalines forced the French to surrender and evacuate the island. Since Leclerc had arrived in Haiti, the French had lost close to 50,000 soldiers and many more were wounded. Bonaparte and Dessalines agreed to a ceasefire, and the French had ten days to leave the island. Rochambeau escaped in defeat and fled back to France. Dessalines created the Haitian flag to represent unity between the Black and biracial population, ordering his army to kill every French person still on the island.

Dessalines proclaimed Haiti's independence and declared Hispaniola the first Black republic in the world. By 1804, Haiti had created its own Constitution, claiming "Independence from all powers of the universe" and abolishing slavery forever. Haiti promised equal treatment under the law, regardless of race and class, whether a citizen or not. They welcomed every Negro around the world and promised them freedom and citizenship. However, no white slave owner from any nation was allowed to set foot on the island. White males weren't even allowed to buy property. They did make an exception for white women, allowing them and their children to be nationalized. Dessalines was crowned emperor, and the Haitians began helping others in the Caribbean take their freedom.

European nations around the world started paying attention to Haiti. To avoid a similar situation, the U.S. Congress forbade slave traders from importing Negros and mulattos into America. Still, South Carolina opened a new slave port and brought slaves in directly from Africa. Many of the French exiled from Haiti came to America, bringing their slave codes with them. When the French arrived, they urged Thomas Jefferson to reduce the number of free Black men in the militia and wanted to decrease the Black population as a whole. After some mixed-race slave owners came to America, they feared another revolution. Many free Negros ended up in New Orleans.

Although America and Thomas Jefferson opposed the Haitian Revolution aiding France and placing sanctions on Haiti, the revolution saved America in more ways than one. Bonaparte planned to conquer America after regaining control of Haiti. He even sent troops to America in preparation. But after losing to Dessalines and the Haitians he was out of soldiers and money.

In 1803, Thomas Jefferson tried to buy New Orleans from France, but Bonaparte refused. After he was defeated by Dessalines, Bonaparte lost so many troops and resources he was forced to give up French land in America. Instead of Jefferson buying New Orleans, Bonaparte offered the entire Louisiana territory for $15 million. The deal doubled the size of America. The territory included Missouri, Arkansas, Oklahoma, Nebraska, Kansas, Wyoming, Colorado, Montana, New Mexico, parts of North and South Dakota, parts of Texas, and parts of Florida.

With the expansion of America, the debate on expanding slavery also intensified. Although Ohio was a free state, laws were passed to discourage free Negros from coming into the colony. To restrict their movement, Black people were required to show proof of freedom to live in the state or seek employment. In New Jersey, a law declared children born to enslaved women before July 4, 1804 were no longer considered slaves but servants, apprenticed for life. Children born to enslaved women after that date still had to serve the owner until the age of 21 for women and 25 for men.

Instead of ending slavery, gradual emancipation laws opened the market for selling and trading pregnant Black women. Enslaved women of childbearing age became priceless. The number of female slaves sold skyrocketed. Many children were sent down South to places like Louisiana. But in 1805, the Virginia legislature voted to create a territory for Freedmen with land received in the Louisiana Purchase. Virginia was also beginning to allow slaves in white churches if they were with their owners. However, they still didn't allow free Blacks in the state.

Benjamin Banneker passed away in 1806. Before he died, he accused Thomas Jefferson of using fraud and violence to oppress his slaves. Backed by several states, Jefferson asked Congress to end the international slave trade. He was aware of the revolution in Haiti and feared the same would happen in America.

Haitians were already helping end slavery in places like Ecuador, Colombia, Venezuela, and the Dominican Republic. Left with no other options, France lobbied England, Spain, and America to isolate and starve Haiti economically. They cut Haiti off from all trading, and European powers did everything they could to hurt them. Jefferson called on Congress to boycott and impose trade embargos. American ships were allowed to go to Haiti, but Haitian ships were forbidden from coming to America. All their governments refused to recognize Haiti's independence.

It wasn't long before Jean-Jacques Dessalines was assassinated. Many believe the French were behind it, with help from America and Britain. Everyone respected Dessalines, and he was able to unify the people, but after his death, the unity left with him. The mulatto class still felt superior and thought Negros should go back to their position as slaves. The two men said to be responsible for Dessalines' death, Alexandre Petion and Henry Christophe, caused even more division after they both crowned themselves king. But even in the middle of a civil war, both groups protected the coastal areas, knowing any European would enslave them all.

By 1807, America was producing 50 million pounds of cotton per year. Yet, with the events in Haiti on their minds, Congress officially banned the slave trade in America, set to take effect on January 1, 1808. Nonetheless, many continued to bring slaves into the country illegally. New York was forced to pass a law prohibiting slaves from being taken out of the state unless they had been with the owner for at least ten years.

As free Black people began migrating to free states, Ohio passed more laws to discourage them from passing through. Many white citizens believed they'd go to Indigenous communities and unite to rise up. To get into Ohio, free Negros were required to post a $500 bond for welfare and security. They also had to get the signature of a white person who agreed to be responsible for them. Additionally, the Negro immigration law forced white residents to comply with the Fugitive Slave Act and the Black Employment Policy. The employment policy required Black people to show freedom papers before being hired.

Once in Ohio, Black people were denied access to public schools, welfare programs, joining the militia, and carrying arms. They were also forbidden from voting, testifying against white people, and serving jury duty. Following suit, New Jersey not only banned Negros from voting, they also took away the woman's right to vote. When the ban on the slave trade officially went into effect, close to 400,000 kidnapped victims were brought to America on record.

America was the only place where the slave population increased, despite banning the slave trade. Owners forced slaves to breed and called it a "natural increase." Although breeding farms already existed, after the slave trade ended, they expanded exponentially. The value of enslaved women of childbearing age skyrocketed, some of them as young as 12.

The two largest breeding farms were in Maryland and Richmond, VA. Most of these plantations were full of enslaved women and children. There were only a few male slaves, and they were expected to get at least 12 women pregnant per year. A slave named Burt fathered over 200 children alone. The bodies of boys were inspected at a young age to determine if they'd be breeders. If they were deemed unworthy, they were often castrated and forced to work on the farm or were sold.

Black men and boys were put through a process known as buck

breaking. Slavers often targeted the biggest, strongest man, or anyone rebellious, to send a message. They tied the naked captive and forced another slave to whip them until they were told to stop. After they were beaten, the owner raped them in front of everyone, including their wife and children. Then other homosexual white males took turns raping them. Sometimes, owners forced other male slaves to rape them, threatening the same punishment if they didn't comply.

They also raped men and women on slave ships. Jamaica may have had the most breeding farms and buck breaking plantations. Buck breaking in Jamaica was so rampant, Jamaicans shun homosexuality to this day. Many slave owners in Jamaica and America were homosexual and often molested little boys. They believed one of a slave's functions was to give pleasure to their owner.

The wives and daughters of slave owners participated in rape culture as well. If a male slave refused to have sex, white women often threatened to yell rape if they didn't get what they wanted. White women also forced male slaves to rape Black women as punishment or for breeding. When white women became pregnant, they often forced Black women to get pregnant at the same time in order to breastfeed their children.

On breeding farms, they put bags over the slaves' heads so they wouldn't know who they were having sex with. They forced them to breed with their cousins, aunts, uncles, and other family members. In some cases, they were even forced to breed with their sister or mother.

Some say that's where the term "motherfucker" originated. The job of castrated slaves was to showcase the women for sale. They were forced to wear dresses to further emasculate them as they presented the women. As the original pimps in America, slave owners sold sexual access to slaves, including for reproduction. Black girls were required to have children when they hit puberty. By the time they were 20, they were expected to have at least four children. To encourage women to have as many children as possible, they promised freedom to women with at least 15 children. However, they rarely kept their word.

In many cases, enslaved women were impregnated by their owners, causing white women to become extremely jealous and angry. Some of them even beheaded mixed-race children, especially if it was their husband's child. But certain owners forced slaves to have orgies in front of them for entertainment. Sometimes they even joined in. Too often when we talk about rape culture, we overlook white women's roles in that very culture.

In 1809, New York recognized marriage between Black people, including slaves. That year, James Madison was elected the fourth president of America and was the third to own slaves while in office. When the third U.S. Census was taken in 1810, Black people made up 19 percent of the population. There were 186,500 free Negros, but nearly 1.2 million were enslaved. Georgia and South Carolina alone produced 60 million pounds of cotton per year. The demand and price of slaves continued to rise.

To keep up with the demand for cotton and sugar, France was determined to get Haiti back. Bonaparte sent representatives to negotiate with Alexandre Petion who was elected president. Petion agreed to pay an indemnity to France in exchange for recognition as an independent nation. Most of the slave owners in Haiti left for America. Their brutal style of slavery led to the Louisiana Uprising of 1811.

The uprising began on the Andry plantation. A slave named Charles Deslondes led a group of slaves armed with machetes and axes into the big house. They severely injured the owner, but he survived. However, his son was killed in his sleep. Fifteen more slaves joined them as they marched towards New Orleans. Along the way, they burned every plantation they came across and recruited more rebels. After marching for two days, their numbers grew to around 500. When the governor became aware, he sent in the militia to stop them.

The militia found them with assistance from Indian trackers and dogs. But with a mindset of freedom, the rebels continued to march, chanting "liberty or death." Outmanned and outgunned, the rebels were ultimately defeated. Charles Deslondes was eventually captured and tortured to send a message to others. They chopped off his hands and shot him in each leg repeatedly until they were broken, then continued to shoot up the rest of his body. Before Charles died, they put his body in a bundle of hay and set it on fire, just so others could hear him scream.

The next day, two more slaves, Pierre Griffee and Hans Wimprenn, were also accused of murder. Although neither of them had a trial, their heads were cut off and placed on spikes as a warning. Eighteen others were granted a trial, but they were all convicted and sentenced to death by a firing squad. In another set of trials, eleven more were convicted, and three of them were publicly hung. In accordance with the law, owners of anyone executed or killed in battle were compensated with $300 for each slave they lost. In response, Louisiana began using federal troops to discourage or stop any more resistance.

By 1811, Paul Cuffee took his first trip to Sierra Leone. It led to the first Black-initiated Back to Africa Movement in America. At the time, Paul may have been the wealthiest Black person in America. He was the first free Black man to have an audience with the president inside The White House. Paul intended to establish a colony for Black people around the world. After founding the Friendly Society of Sierra Leone, he planned to send two ships per year to take Black people in America to the colony. However, on a trip in 1812, U.S. Customs stopped Paul and seized his property. James Madison supported Paul's Back to Africa movement, but for different reasons. Madison met with Paul and had his property returned.

Paul traveled to Baltimore, Philadelphia, and New York to form an organization called the African Institution. Since many states banned free Negros, the emigration movement became popular among the free, rich Black population. After Louisiana was admitted into the Union, there were eight slave states and eight free states.

Historically speaking, Europeans have always had trouble accepting defeat. Britain was no different. After the Revolutionary War, they continued attacking American ships and attempted to block trade between America and other countries. France and Britain were already at war, and Britain feared America would support the French. Britain began funding native rebels to fight against America, expanding into their territories. Eventually, in 1812, James Madison signed America's first declaration of war against Britain and Ireland.

America's goal was to conquer and expand into Canada, which Britain also controlled. Native tribes like the Shawnee tribe, led by Chief Tecumseh, met their plans to expand west and north with resistance.

Many tribes lost most of their land by signing treaties with America.

Tecumseh refused but America wouldn't take no for an answer. They attacked the natives, burning their villages to the ground. Although Indians are known for scalping people today, American troops were scalping Indigenous tribes first.

Aware of America's plan to invade Canada, Britain formed an alliance with native tribes. People like Tecumseh helped the British take American land, including Detroit. Using propaganda, any time colonizers win a battle, it's called a great success. Anytime they lose, it's called a massacre.

Tecumseh believed in the rules of warfare and was against harming women or children. He even adopted young white children and assimilated them into their culture. As usual, Britain betrayed Tecumseh, leaving him to fight alone. Eventually, he was defeated and killed in battle. American soldiers stripped and scalped his body before peeling off his skin to take as souvenirs.

After the War of 1812, Indian nations signed over 200 treaties, giving up most of their land. Reservations were created west of the Mississippi, but Indigenous tribes could no longer be a part of America. Similar to the Revolutionary War, during the War of 1812, Britain offered slaves freedom in exchange for joining their army. Once again, America was forced to make the same offer to have any chance of winning the war. However, many white citizens were angry and petitioned against arming Negros, claiming it put slave owners in danger.

The war lasted until 1814, when the Treaty of Ghent was signed. America agreed to stop invading Canada if Britain stopped offering slaves freedom. Incidentally, in one of the last battles, a slave owner, Francis Scott Key, wrote a poem America made its national anthem. In the third verse of the Star-Spangled Banner, Key talked about killing any slave who sided with the British, although they were only fighting for their freedom as well.

Francis Key was a lawyer and often persecuted abolitionists and owners trying to free their slaves. He even called for someone to be hung just for having an anti-slavery pamphlet. Yet to this day, Black Americans still don't have the freedom to respond to or protest the national anthem.

People like Colin Kaepernick and Shareef Abdur-Rahim were blackballed from their careers within a year for not standing for the anthem to protest injustices.

After America won its independence for the second time, Britain was done for good.

Black soldiers who sided with the British were forced to leave. Many of them settled in Trinidad and Nova Scotia. Those who chose to fight for America didn't fare much better, as it didn't make whites less angry. In fact, the thought of Black gun ownership, Black unity, and freedom enraged and scared them more. For the second time, America was forced to beg Negros to help them win a war. And for the second time, Negros were betrayed.

CHAPTER 9.
SEARCHING FOR FREEDOM: THE
FIRST SEMINOLE WAR

America was officially liberated from Britain and sought to ensure that "the land of the free and home of the brave" concept only applied to one group. When America needed Black soldiers, some states, including New York, extended the right to jury trials to slaves. But after the British agreed to stop offering freedom, they returned to their normal practices. Free biracial communities that were established in Spanish Florida were destroyed. They were seen as a threat that would eventually challenge the white status quo.

As president, Thomas Jefferson preached against racial amalgamation, despite having four children with Sally Hemings. Colonizers used phrases like "crossing blood" as rhetoric to stop whites from having sex with Negros. Jefferson didn't feel the same about Indigenous people, especially those with lighter skin. He said, "The Indians would come to identify with whiteness, and children mixed with Indian and white blood would align with the superior white blood." Jefferson even wrote a letter expressing regret about the war because it stopped the "amalgamation with the Indians," and thought they should be one people.

On the other hand, he wrote against mixing blood with Negros because it led to white degradation. He said, "No lover of his country, no lover of excellence in the human character can innocently consent." Jefferson was a hypocrite and "amalgamated" with Negros himself. He understood Black blood would eventually wash out white blood.

A Virginia congressman, John Randolph, tried to propose a bill to end slavery in DC altogether, but it didn't pass. However, the king of the Netherlands ended Dutch participation in the slave trade in 1814 but gave no date on when it would go into effect. The institution of slavery itself continued in the Netherlands.

In 1815, a white abolitionist named George Boxley attempted to start an uprising known as The Boxley Slave Rebellion in Spotsylvania, VA. He planned to organize captives and take over Fredericksburg and Richmond. However, a slave named Lucy told authorities about the plan. Boxley was arrested along with 27 slaves who were suspected of being involved. Six slaves were executed, and five others were shipped out of Virginia. Although Boxley was the leader, he was only sentenced to jail. He escaped but was captured before escaping again.

Boxley was banned from Virginia and wanted by bounty hunters but was never found. Meanwhile, in 1815, Paul Cuffe took 38 free Negros back to Sierra Leone on his second trip. In Philadelphia, 16 Black churches united to establish the African Methodist Episcopal Church. The A.M.E. church was created to push education for Black people and served as a station for the Underground Railroad. In 1816, Robert Finley established the American Colonization Society, although he had completely different motivations than Paul Cuffe. Finley wanted to kick free Negros out of the country and send them to Liberia, but he had no interest in ending the institution of slavery.

Finley met with prominent members, including Francis Scott Key, John Randolph, Thomas Jefferson, Andrew Jackson, and James Monroe, all of whom owned slaves. The Colonization Society wasn't officially absolved until 1964. In 1817, as protests to abolish slavery expanded, New York was forced to set a date within 10 years to free anyone still enslaved. That year, Frederick Douglass was born enslaved on a plantation in Maryland. Samuel Ringgold Ward was also born enslaved in Maryland, but he escaped with his parents at the age of three.

After the War of 1812, many slaves in Maryland realized they weren't going to get the freedom they were promised. Free Blacks also realized they'd never be accepted or treated fairly under the law. They felt they were out of options. One day, around 200 slaves attacked white residents with sticks and whatever they could find. The militia was eventually called in to stop the attack, but white abolitionists blamed it on the Colonization Society and free Negros.

In 1817, Georgia banned interstate slave trading because they felt it was too dangerous to let Negros communicate on a global scale. In

Florida, Andrew Jackson began leading raids on free Black communities. Jackson gained fame during the War of 1812. His goal was to break up Black communities and re-enslave or kill as many people as he could. Jackson took military posts and eventually gained control of Pensacola.

The Fort Blount Rebellion had already occurred by 1816 when 300 slaves took over Fort Blount for a few days. Jackson's army eventually took Fort Blount back before burning it down and killing every slave. As Jackson attacked Negros in Florida, James Monroe was elected the fifth president and was the fourth to own slaves. Monroe was a leader in the Colonization Society and played a key role in seizing land in Africa to create Liberia. The capital, Monrovia, was named after him.

Before James Madison left office, he admitted Mississippi into the Union in 1817. Under the Ordinance of 1787, Mississippi was able to legalize slavery since Indiana was admitted as a free state. During a court case, Harry v. Decker and Hopkins, the Supreme Court of Mississippi ruled that slaves brought into Indiana were to be set free. Harry sued for his freedom with two others after being moved from Virginia. Many free states, like Illinois, opposed emancipating slaves if they were brought into the state. Even in the North, Philadelphia passed legislation to establish a plan to educate poor children, but it excluded Black children. Before the first Black school was built in 1829, they were forced to learn while piled into cramped rooms.

Connecticut also did what it could to discourage free Blacks from coming. Before 1818, free Black property owners could vote, but the new state constitution limited voting to white male property owners 21 and over, with at least $7 worth of property. Free Blacks petitioned the General Assembly to exempt them from taxes since they couldn't vote. The assembly rejected the petition and forced them to pay taxes, including a poll tax, despite Blacks not being allowed to vote.

In 1819, America signed the Adams-Onis Treaty with Spain. America gained control over Florida in exchange for five million dollars, and Spain agreed to stop expanding into Texas territory. James Monroe said since the Spanish couldn't stop runaway slaves from invading American territory to free their people, Spain owed them. Essentially, America acquired Florida for free. One of the few places where slaves had a chance for freedom was officially controlled by America and Andrew Jackson.

Virginia decided to pass the Revised Code of 1819, which considered free Negros or mulattos meeting anywhere, including their homes, unlawful assembly. Despite being free, they were forbidden from learning how to read and write. If anyone was caught teaching others, they were punished at the discretion of the sworn "peace" officer. However, the punishment couldn't exceed 20 lashes.

Although America already banned the slave trade, many still transported slaves illegally.

Attempting to crack down on the illegal trade, Congress passed laws making it a felony to smuggle in slaves. The president had the power to send slaves illegally imported back to Africa or send armed ships there if needed. In response, Virginia and North Carolina repealed laws against interstate slave trading. Richmond, VA, became a major hub for the slave market.

Since Florida was no longer an option for slaves, the Underground Railroad expanded. Canada denied America the right to pursue slaves who crossed the border. As Alabama was admitted into the Union as the 22nd state and the 11th slave state, the crackdown on runaway slaves increased. South Carolina passed a law making it illegal to distribute any anti-slavery literature in the state. Instead of running to the South to find freedom, slaves began heading North.

South Carolina experienced several uprisings. In 1816, a group of slaves planned a revolt known as the Camden Slave Rebellion. They planned to strike on the 4th of July, and armed themselves while whites were celebrating their independence day. Knowing they'd be drunk, they saw it as their best chance to escape. However, a slave named Scipio informed his owner of the plan. They hung six captives suspected of being involved in front of the town. White residents claimed the plan was to kill all the white males and rape every white woman before destroying the city. They also convicted another slave named Stephen, and he was to be hung.

But for some reason, they released him after everyone else was executed. Scipio was rewarded with his freedom and $50 a year for life.

Undeterred, the number of rebellions increased. The same year as the Camden rebellion, an uprising was also planned in Fredericksburg, VA. They were likewise betrayed, and the leaders were hung. But white fear increased, and once again, they falsely accused the perpetrators of planning to kill every white male. They killed many of those who were accused without evidence, justifying it by saying they stopped the rebellion before it happened.

In Augusta, GA, rumors of an uprising led to a slave named Coot being executed in 1819. Slaves were tortured into false confessions. A captive named Paul was whipped over 250 times within a month until he said he was involved. At this point, if something caught on fire, a Black person would be blamed and hung. Savannah, GA, punished white residents who taught Negros or mulattos how to read with a $30 fine. Any Negro or mulatto caught teaching others were fined $30, imprisoned for 30 days, and received 39 lashes, even if they owned a school.

Savannah increased their slave patrols by paying any white resident who volunteered $1 per night. Both free and enslaved Blacks were restricted from trading goods or gathering for religious purposes. Additionally, whites could enter or search the home of any Black person at any time.

America wasn't the only place where slaves were uprising. After the Haitian Revolution, the energy of rebellion spread globally. A freedman named Jose Aponte and three others led the largest revolt in Cuban history. Many colonists wanted to make Cuba the leading producer of sugar after losing Haiti. Jose and the others planned to use the same tactics as the Haitians to free every slave on the island. They marched through Havana, going from plantation to plantation, freeing any slave who wanted to join them.

When they got to the third plantation, they were confronted and eventually defeated in battle. But the colonizers realized it was just the first stage in a larger plan to end slavery in Cuba. Jose used drawings and pictures as a form of his own propaganda. He taught people history and showed them how to organize and fight during battle. They found his book with pictures of powerful Black men and destroyed it quickly. Jose was arrested and given a trial, only to question him about the meaning of his drawings. He was sentenced to death by public hanging, and he was decapitated, his head placed on a spike for all to see.

A few years later, a slave named Bussa led another uprising known as Bussa's Rebellion. With the help of a woman named Nanny Grigg and enslaved elders, Bussa expected to take control of the island, since they heavily outnumbered Europeans. He had more privileges than others, with more freedom to move around. This allowed him to communicate and organize. Bussa also knew how to read and write. He planned to organize close to 400 people to strike on Easter Sunday.

They began on the Bayley plantation, catching the British off guard. Over 70 plantations were destroyed in the first few days. The revolt lasted three days, but only two slave owners were killed. The British promised a few slaves freedom and equal protection under the law if they fought against the rebels. At least 40 rebels were killed during the battle. Although over 1,300 people joined the rebellion, they were severely outgunned and were ultimately defeated. Nearly 1,000 rebels were killed, and another 214 were captured and executed. Further, 123 more were arrested and shipped off the island. Bussa died on the battlefield, fighting for freedom.

Although Haitians were able to drive out their oppressors, the colorism civil war continued. At one point, Haiti was divided into four nations. In 1820, Jean Pierre Boyer, the biracial leader, took over the North and eventually controlled the entire island. Boyer was able to reunite the island under the new Republican Constitution of the South, but under the mulatto class. Boyer reached out to Black people in America and invited them to come to Haiti. He even offered to pay for the trip, give them three acres of land, provide ten pounds of coffee per family, and offered monetary rewards.

An estimated 13,000 took the trip to Haiti. Some stayed, but many eventually left due to cultural differences and prejudice from mixed-race Haitian elites. It wasn't long before the country rescinded the offer. Although Haiti was the first Black nation after colonization, it was controlled by biracial elites.

In South Africa, Britain declared formal control over the Cape Colony in 1815. However, in 1816, Shaka Zulu led the rise of the powerful Zulu kingdom in South Africa. After Shaka's father died, he took over the Zulus by force. Shaka was a powerful warrior who brought his mindset to the nation at a time Europeans were moving into the territory. Under his command, the army grew from 400 to 40,000 troops in just a few years.

After defeating neighboring tribes in battle, the Zulu nation was comprised of hundreds of chiefdoms. Shaka's reign only lasted 12 years before he was assassinated. During his rule, he kept the British out of the territory, except on rare occasions when he allowed them to enter for medical reasons. He let certain Europeans stay to show them gratitude for introducing him to medical practices. However, they tried to exploit Shaka and used his kindness to set up invasions later. On his deathbed, he warned the Zulu kingdom they'd fall to the white man that came from the sea.

Back in America, according to the fourth Census in 1820, Black people made up 18 percent of the population. There were over 1.5 million slaves compared to 233,500 free Blacks. Thanks to the Fugitive Slave Act, many free Negros weren't safe either. So many were kidnapped, especially children, that Ohio passed a law making it a misdemeanor to kidnap a free Negro or mulatto and hold them with the intent of transport out of state without a court order.

Anyone convicted had to serve no less than a year in jail, but no more than ten. They could still kidnap and hold free Blacks, but they'd have to go in front of a judge before selling them into a slave state.

In Charleston, S.C., slaves were forced to wear I.D. tags, identifying them as property.

The law also forced free Negros to always carry freedom papers. James Monroe signed an executive order to ban Negros and mulattos from serving in the army. The last thing they wanted was to arm Black people. As white fear increased, Congress passed a law that considered any participation in the slave trade an act of conspiracy.

As 86 Black Americans arrived in Liberia, Congress passed the Missouri Compromise in 1820. Two years earlier, Missouri had petitioned to enter the Union as a slave state. The North objected because the balance of power would go to slave states. Eventually, Maine was split from Massachusetts and admitted into the Union as a free state, so the power remained balanced. The compromise also outlawed slavery north of 36°, 30', or the Mason-Dixon line. The line split Northern and

Southern colonies effectively, but gave slaves hope for freedom if they could make it to the North. In Boston, MA, state-sponsored schools for Black children were created, although they were severely underfunded.

Meanwhile, Spain's government abolished the slave trade south of the equator, but slavery continued in places like Cuba. In 1821, the great warrior and hero Harriet Tubman was born on a plantation in Maryland. Born as Araminta Ross, she was subject to extremely harsh treatment as a child. From the age of six, she was rented out to work for others and beaten constantly.

When Harriet got older, she was leased out to be a nursemaid and forced to take care of white children. She had to stay up all night so the baby wouldn't cry and wake the mother. If she fell asleep, the mother whipped her. By the age of 11, as was custom, Harriet had to wear bright bandanas to show she wasn't a child anymore. She was sexually assaulted constantly and often beaten by jealous white women. When Harriet was 12, she suffered a major brain injury after an overseer hit her in the head for not helping catch a runaway slave. After her injury, Harriet said she received visions she called signs from God.

After the Missouri Compromise was ratified, Missouri was officially admitted into the Union as a slave state. A provision was included that required citizens to return runaway slaves. In Texas, an American slave owner was allowed to start a colony, although the territory was still part of Mexico. The country didn't gain independence until after the Mexican War of Independence. In 1822, Mexico declared itself an independent Catholic nation. Meanwhile, the Dominican Republic also declared its independence from Spain. After Jean Pierre Boyer marched his army into Santo Domingo, he unified both territories and gained control over all of Hispaniola. What the Haitians didn't know was Boyer was already in negotiations with France. The French had been attacking Haiti since the revolution.

In Liberia, the Colonization Society officially took control and planned to ship every free Black person in America there. Liberia was still under American law, and residents still paid taxes. As free Black people searched for a place to call home, many free states passed more Black Codes.

Chicago was founded by a biracial man named Jean Baptiste Point du Sable. He was the first to set up an extensive and prosperous trading settlement in the area. Jean passed away in 1818, and by 1819, Illinois passed its first Black Codes, although it was a free state. Negros were prohibited from voting, testifying against or suing whites, and from gathering in groups of three or more. They were also forbidden from joining the militia or owning firearms. Anyone caught breaking the law was beaten and arrested. Free Blacks were required to carry freedom papers, or they were assumed to be slaves.

The Black Codes and the Fugitive Slave Acts led to countless Black men, women, and children being kidnapped and sold into slavery. By 1822, those who were pro-slavery pushed for it to be legalized nationally. Their proposal was rejected, but the Black Codes were in full effect. Places like Connecticut defined freedmen as white to prevent Black landowners from voting. A successful Black businessman, William Lanson, was denied the right to vote, despite owning property. By 1821, Massachusetts and New York removed property requirements for white males to vote. Free Negros eligible to vote in Rhode Island were also disenfranchised.

In 1822, a free Black man named Samuel Cornish established the first Black Presbyterian Church in New York. Samuel went on to create the Freedom's Journal but later changed the name to The Rights of All. At the same time, white officials in South Carolina began shutting down Black churches. Churches were the only place enslaved and free Blacks could meet and socialize, but many whites saw it as a threat. For some Blacks, the church was their only salvation, and shutting them down was the final straw.

CHAPTER 10.
DENMARK'S REBELLION: THE SECOND MIDDLE PASSAGE

Colonizers used religion as a major tool, but they were also afraid of slaves practicing the very religion forced on them. Denmark Vesey was one of the founders of the African Methodist Episcopal Church in South Carolina in 1818. The church had a congregation with about 1,848 members who were majority Black. Denmark was born in St. Thomas but was shipped to South Carolina after being sold as a child. He worked for the captain of a ship for 19 years until he became a house slave.

Denmark worked on slave ships sometimes, but he had more freedom to move around than others. In 1800, he purchased his freedom for $600 and began working as an independent carpenter. Despite owning a business, like many free Negros, he was still disenfranchised and treated as a second-class human. After white officials shut down Black churches in Charleston, S.C., Denmark decided enough was enough. The Black population heavily outnumbered whites. But free Negros were forced to step off the sidewalk when someone white walked by. It was a crime to even look them in the eye.

Denmark united free and enslaved Negros easily with a plan set to take place on July 14, 1822. At the sound of the church bells, the governor and mayor were supposed to be killed in their sleep by slaves. They were going to break into the armory and take as many weapons as they could carry. They planned to poison the water supply, set fires, and cause explosions all over the city. After killing every white man, woman, and child, they would take the harbor to seize ships and escape to Haiti.

Some say Denmark organized close to 9,000 people. He used his church to hold meetings and prepare others to fight. All it took to get Denmark arrested was one slave going back to tell his master. During his trial, Denmark was asked, "As a free man with a successful business, why would you lead a rebellion?" They used a forced confession from an associate of Denmark, after torturing him for hours. No one testified against Denmark, nor did they find any weapons he was accused of having.

When questioned, Denmark responded by reading Bible quotes from Exodus 21:16, Joshua 6:21, and Zechariah 14:1-2. Over 150 slaves were arrested. Seventy-seven were found guilty, forty-two were deported, and thirty-five were hung. The platform was so high that they were choked by the noose but didn't die. The executioner went down the line, shooting them in the head one by one. Their bodies were chopped up and left out in public to send a message to others.

After Denmark's rebellion, South Carolina tightened their slave codes. All Negro gatherings were prohibited unless supervised by someone white. Curfews were enforced to restrict Black people from moving around freely. South Carolina also passed the Seamen's Act and arrested Black sailors until they left the state. The ship's captain paid the cost to jail Black sailors. If he didn't pay, they could be sold into slavery. South Carolina feared Blacks would spread Denmark's story and send messages in and out of the state.

Initially, Denmark tried to buy his wife and children's freedom. Their owners refused to sell them at any price because Denmark was a Negro. Moreover, whites wanted something done about the free Black population because they were afraid they'd help others get freedom. A major part of Denmark's motivation was to free his family. But whites wanted to bury the memory of Denmark Vesey as fast as possible and tore down the church, brick by brick.

The spirit of rebellion wasn't only in America or Haiti, it spread throughout the diaspora. In Demerara, now Guyana, sugar plantations were losing value as demand decreased. To make up for the profit, slaves worked even harder to produce more sugar. But slaves quickly grew tired of the extra labor and decided to fight back. In 1823, around 9,000 slaves organized to start the Demerara Rebellion. They were led by Jack Gladstone and his father Quamina, along with several others.

Quamina was against bloodshed and suggested a boycott until new laws were passed.

Many enslaved people disagreed and felt violence was the only answer. Some slaves were loyal to their owners, and others said they were Christian and refused to be involved. A house slave named Joseph Packwood warned his owner about the revolt, but it was too late. Many slaves took firearms from their plantations and locked up their owners during the night. They didn't even demand freedom; they only asked for better treatment.

The governor met them on the street with the militia. They only demanded basic human rights, but the governor refused to listen. He ordered them to go back to their plantations. When they refused, the militia opened fire and killed around 200 people. Some went back to their plantations, but the shooting motivated nearly 11,000 slaves on over 55 plantations to fight back. After a few whites were killed, the governor declared martial law. The rebellion lasted for two days, but the rebels were outgunned, and whites didn't let Christianity stop them from spilling their blood.

After the battle, they lined up the bodies of the rebels and decapitated them. They placed their severed heads on pikes and left them on public roads for all to see. Hundreds of people were hunted down and slaughtered. Others were arrested and sentenced to be hung. Some of the rebels, including Jack Gladstone, were shipped off the island. Although Quamina was against bloodshed, he was tracked down by dogs and Indigenous trackers and killed.

After Chile officially abolished slavery in 1823, the U.S. Congress cut funding to stop the slave trade. After Denmark used the Bible to inspire the people, two white priests, Frederick Dalcho and Richard Furman, urged religious instructors and slave owners to use the Bible to teach slaves to respect their masters. They suggested instead of taking the Bible away from Negros, they should take measures to ensure slaves read only what they wanted them to read.

Mississippi outlawed teaching slaves how to read and write completely in 1823. However, Alexander Lucius Twilight graduated from Middlebury College that year. He was the first Black college graduate in America. But Louisiana didn't take long to pass harsher slave laws with the Civil Code of 1824. The Civil Code defined a slave as "one who is in the power of a master to whom he belongs." It also stated, "The master may sell him or dispose of him or his industry and his labor." Slaves were also forbidden from owning or acquiring anything unless it was for their owner. The only thing an enslaved person could keep was the money they earned. But they couldn't enter any contracts unless it was for freedom, and only if the owner allowed it.

Of course, slaves weren't allowed to hold any public office. They were also forbidden from becoming an attorney, an executioner, or a teacher. They also weren't allowed to be a witness or involved in any court case, unless it was for their freedom. Additionally, Louisiana no longer recognized slave marriages unless they had permission from their owners. Nor could they pass down any possessions to their children. Even when owners wanted to emancipate a slave, it was prohibited until the slave turned 30 and had at least four years of "good behavior." These were only a few of the laws South Carolina passed with the Civil Code.

However, a nine year old Henry Highland Garnet escaped with his family after attending a funeral. After becoming an activist, Abraham Lincoln invited him to speak in the House of Representatives making him the first Black person to address the legislature. In Henry's speech, "Call to Rebellion," he encouraged slaves to free themselves by rising against owners.

In 1824, Indiana passed laws to make it a little more difficult to enforce the Fugitive Slave Act, although many were still being kidnapped. Mexico also passed laws to ban the slave trade after the first and only Black president, Vicente Guerrero, took office in 1824. Vicente was a leader in the fight against the Spanish. He became known as the liberator of Mexico. The Spanish wanted to keep the "pure blood" caste system, but Black, biracial, and native Mexicans united to fight against it.

After the Haitian Revolution, European powers, led by France, Britain, and America, placed embargos and other restrictions on Haiti. Despite winning their independence, whites refused to recognize Haiti as a free nation. With warships ready to fire, France returned in 1825. They threatened to reinstate slavery if Haiti didn't pay $150 million in gold francs as reparations. France claimed they were owed for all the slaves and land they lost. They took advantage of the colorism civil wars, and Haiti was unable to defend itself. Haiti was forced to pay France for freedom. In addition to money, France also demanded a 50 percent discount on exported goods.

The first payment Haiti made in 1825 was $24 million in gold francs. In 1838, France reduced the debt to $90 million in gold francs to be paid over 30 years. In return, France agreed to stop invading and recognized Haiti as an independent nation. With the country divided and decimated, Jean Pierre Boyer figured he had no choice but to agree. It took Haiti until 1947, but they paid every cent of "reparations" to France. It was financed by French banks along with the American Citibank.

After paying France, Haiti was destroyed economically and is still struggling to recover today. They gained their freedom, but at what cost? France, America, and other European nations continued to interfere with Haiti's economic growth and occupied land anytime they wanted. To this day, embargos and restrictions are placed on Haiti, making it difficult to export goods. Haiti was the most profitable colony, but after taking their freedom, Europeans globally set out to destroy it.

Back in America, a white woman named Frances "Fanny" Wright wanted to create what she called a "Utopian Society" for free Negros. She planned to organize a group of slaves to work together and make enough money to buy each other's freedom. Wright built the community in Germantown, TN, near Memphis, and named it Nashoba. But only white residents could manage the community. At its largest, it had no more than 20 members and got a reputation for being a "free love society." It caused more financial problems and Nashoba collapsed within two years.

In New York, free Black clergymen published A Remonstrance Against the Abuse of Blacks in 1826. The General Colored Association was also founded that year in Massachusetts. Still, states like Pennsylvania were forced to pass more laws against free Blacks, especially children, being kidnapped. Without an official certificate of removal, it was a felony to remove a slave from the state. Abolitionists created the Free Produce Society of Pennsylvania to encourage people to not buy goods produced by slave labor.

Thomas Jefferson died in 1826. Before he died, Jefferson planned to buy enslaved children and send them to Haiti instead of just freeing them. Although some claim Jefferson opposed slavery, after he died, only five of his slaves were freed. The other 130 slaves were sold to pay his debt. Not even Sally Hemmings was freed, despite having multiple children with Jefferson. By 1825, John Quincy Adams was elected the sixth president. Adams was only the second president that didn't own slaves. Some say he was also against slavery, but he respected slave owners and their "property" rights to the utmost.

After the War of 1812, Adams fought to re-enslave Black soldiers who sided with the British. Ultimately, he won a payout from the British government to compensate slave owners for their loss of property. After a case in 1827, the courts ruled America had to compensate Spain for every slave taken off their ships if they could prove they were going to Spanish territories.

After many decades, New York abolished slavery. But children born to enslaved mothers still had to serve the owner until their 20s. About 10,000 slaves were freed with the New York Emancipation Act, but the 1830 Census reported 75 people were still enslaved. In Maryland, the Baltimore Society for the Protection of Free People of Color was created. The society was established to help free Blacks who were kidnapped and sold into slavery. Although slavery was still legal in Tennessee, slave trading was officially banned in the state.

In Texas, slave trading was still legal in private transactions. However, Texas required owners to free 10 percent of the slaves they inherited. Although Texas was still supposed to be a part of Mexico, in 1829, Mexico issued a decree to "free all slaves forever." It wasn't long before Mexico became a refuge for enslaved people. Mexico granted Texas and U.S. citizens exemption and allowed them to continue practicing slavery.

Today, many argue few whites owned slaves. But many poor whites not only felt superior to Negros, they also resented slaves for making it difficult to find work. It wasn't slave owners forming lynch mobs and attacking the Black community. Most times, it was poor white immigrants committing the violence. In August 1829, the Cincinnati race riot started after a mob of 250 whites, mostly Irish, attacked the Black community. They destroyed homes and murdered many innocent people.

Many runaway slaves and free Blacks moved to Ohio, looking for work. Poor whites were angry Negros were taking jobs because they had more skills and were more qualified. Many white residents wanted to enforce a law that was passed in 1807 that required Negros to pay $500 or leave the state within 30 days. Before the 30 days were up, the enraged mob assaulted the Black community from August 15 to 22.

The police didn't stop the violence; in fact, some joined in. Some whites were arrested, but some of the victims were arrested as well. After the attack, half of the Black population left the city. Those who stayed continued to deal with violence. Many left for Canada. There, James Charles Brown, Israel Lewis, and Thomas Crissup were leaders in founding the Wilberforce colony near Ontario.

In Boston, a free Black man named David Walker started publishing his own paper, calling for the unity of Black people worldwide. An Appeal to the Colored People of the World was about organizing to take military action against slavery, racism, and white supremacy. In New York, another free Black man named Robert Alexander Young published The Ethiopian Manifesto: Issued in Defense of the Black Man's Rights in the Scale of Universal Freedom.

David Walker and others used writing to advocate for ending slavery and gaining equal rights by any means necessary. But laws became harsher for both free and enslaved Negros in slave states. In Georgia, any white person caught teaching a Negro how to read or write was fined $500 and faced imprisonment. Black teachers could be fined as well, but most times, they were whipped. In Louisiana, the punishment for teaching a slave how to read was a year in jail. A father or mother could be flogged for teaching their own children how to read and write.

Often, the punishment for Negros who were caught reading was much worse than being whipped. Some had their eyes gouged out, their tongue removed, or their limbs amputated. In North Carolina, after a Supreme Court case, State v. Mann, the court declared chattel slaves had no rights and slave owners had full dominion over their slaves' lives. According to the North Carolina Supreme Court, no slave could have a will of their own.

The case was over an enslaved woman named Lydia. She had tried to run away after being severely beaten by her owner, John Mann. When Lydia attempted to escape, Mann shot her. Lydia survived but was severely injured. The shooting was deemed excessive, and Mann was arrested for assault and battery. However, the judge, Thomas Ruffin, ruled the power of the master must be absolute to render submission of the perfect slave. Inhumane punishments for slaves were officially deemed legal in North Carolina.

To make matters worse, Andrew Jackson was elected the seventh president of America and was the fifth slave owner. Jackson owned over 200 slaves and was involved in slave trading as well. The fifth Census in 1830 showed Black people made up 18 percent of the population.

There were around 319,500 free Blacks, but over 2 million were enslaved. Most of the free Black population lived in New York, Boston, and Philadelphia. Eventually, the first Negro Convention was held in Philadelphia in 1830, from September 20 to 24. There, they debated if free Blacks should leave the country for Canada. Although the Colonization Society sent 529 people to Liberia, many free Blacks didn't trust them and didn't want to be under their rule.

Not long after Andrew Jackson got into office, he passed the Indian Removal Act of 1830. Jackson planned to take land from native tribes east of the Mississippi. The Choctaws were the first to sign a treaty, forcing them to leave the land. Of course, America has broken most of the treaties they've signed. But native tribes were forced out of Georgia, Alabama, North Carolina, Florida, and Tennessee so whites could move in. Many know about the Trail of Tears, but very few talk about the slave's Trail of Tears.

By 1830, the U.S. was producing 331 million pounds of cotton. Jackson and other whites wanted the land and access to cotton fields. Thousands of slaves were sent to replace the native population in what some called the Second Middle Passage. Between 1830 and 1860, thousands of enslaved men, women, and children were marched hundreds of miles in chains. The expression, "sold down the river" comes from this time. Stories of children being ripped from their mothers and entire families being separated became even more common than before.

As the demand for slaves increased, the prices rose from $500 in 1800 to about $1,800 in 1860. In 1830, Louisiana also passed more laws to prevent slaves from learning how to read and write. Yet, Louisiana's legislature complained to Congress that too many slaves were escaping to Mexico. Mexico decided to end white immigration into Texas and forbade any more slaves from being imported. However, by 1829, the first and only Black President of Mexico, Vicente Guerrero was ousted by the government after returning from the Mexican War of Independence.

Many Mexican elitists feared Vicente because he was a descendant of Aztec royalty. They certainly didn't want a darker-skinned leader, fearing he'd appeal to native Mexicans. They also feared Vincente would appeal to those of mixed-race and destroy the race-based caste system. His vice president, Anastasio Bustamante, had more Spanish blood and lighter skin.

Bustamante led a rebellion against Vicente after the Congress of Mexico declared him incapable of leading. Bustamante became acting president. Vicente was eventually betrayed, captured, and executed by a firing squad in 1831.

Too often, Black leaders aren't just taken out of power, they are killed. Within a year of David Walker's call for global unity, he was mysteriously found dead. His message not only got the attention of Black people, but struck fear in whites as well. Some even offered rewards for his death. Many of David's family and friends tried to convince him to leave for Canada, but he refused to run away or back down. Although he was only 33, many said he died from natural causes. Some claimed he may have had tuberculosis because his daughter died from it.

However, those close to David assumed someone poisoned him and felt the police covered it up, or at the least didn't investigate. By 1831, the Colonization Society moved South to open a chapter in Mississippi. In New England, the Massachusetts Anti-Slavery Society was also formed. More organizations strictly for Black women were created as well. Both the African American Female Society in Boston and the Colored Female Society in Philadelphia were established for free Black women.

Across America, the term "Underground Railroad" was used to describe the process for runaway slaves escaping to freedom. They often used songs to communicate with each other in code. Black leaders with independent thought have always been a threat to this system. A Black person with power, be it with a gun, a pen, or a voice, is not only a target, but the system also tries to erase them from history completely—not only to instill fear and submission of slaves, but to keep Black people from unifying to fight back. White supremacy can only be defined by Black inferiority.

CHAPTER 11.
JUMP JIM CROW: NAT TURNER'S REVOLT

Despite being hated and classified as subhuman, there has always been a fascination with Black people and our culture. During the 1830s and '40s, white actors used blackface to mock Black people for entertainment. Europeans portrayed Black caricatures as early as 1604. By 1690, even dancing was outlawed for slaves. They often shuffled and glided their feet to avoid breaking the law. Many of the first actors in minstrel shows, known as Ethiopian delineators, were Irish and Jewish immigrants making fun of the way Blacks walked and talked.

At the time, neither Irish nor Jewish people were considered white. Often, non-white groups disparaged Black people to be accepted and earn their whiteness. Thomas Dartmouth Rice became known as the father of American minstrelsy. Rice was the first to bring blackface minstrel shows to the New York Theater in 1828. After writing and producing a song and dance called Jim Crow, he became famous for introducing minstrel shows to the masses.

Many Black caricature stereotypes, such as the mammy, the zip coon, the sambo, and more, were created from these shows. Whites paid money to see someone imitate a Black person and believed they were accurate depictions. Many whites had never seen a Black person or were afraid to be around them. This was their way of being entertained by Negros without being near them. By 1843, the shows were spreading across America. Blackface actors eventually came together to form the minstrel circuit.

Frederick Douglass described the shows as "filthy scum of white society, stealing a complexion denied to them by nature to make money and pander to the corrupt taste of fellow white citizens." Minstrel shows portrayed Blacks, including children, as dumb buffoons who were happily enslaved. To them, Negros wanted to be tamed so they wouldn't be savages and brutes. These shows gave them an excuse to be even more racist and still fall asleep at night. As the shows became more popular, images of Black children being eaten by alligators appeared. Some tried to justify using Black babies as alligator bait.

So many children were kidnapped, Ohio passed more laws to forbid taking free Blacks out of the state. In 1831, The Liberator newspaper was created by William Lloyd Garrison.

Garrison was the first to propose the term African American for Black people. Although free Blacks wanted to use logic and reason to end slavery, those who were enslaved were ready to take more urgent actions to acquire freedom.

A few days before Gabriel Prosser's execution, Nat Turner was born enslaved in Southampton, VA. From a young age, Nat had frequent visions he described as messages from God. He learned how to read and write using the Bible, the only book he was allowed to read. Nat escaped slavery when he turned 21. But after a month, he said he received visions telling him to go back and lead the people. After becoming a preacher, slave owners brought Nat in to teach slaves to respect their earthly masters. When they weren't looking, he used the Bible to preach about freedom.

Secretly, Nat Turner planned a revolt, set to take place on July 4, 1831. However, he became ill before it could happen. After an eclipse on August 13, Nat was convinced it was a sign to reschedule the rebellion. On the night of August 21, he and six other slaves killed their owner, Joseph Travis, and his entire family. They also murdered Putnum Moore, Nat's official owner, even though he was a child. After taking guns and horses, they went from plantation to plantation, killing every white man, woman, or child they came across. Along the way, they freed over 70 people.

Nat's group killed at least 60 whites, including babies. Eventually, the militia brought in reinforcements from three different companies and defeated them, killing at least 100 people. Another 56 were executed by the state, whether they were involved or not. Word of the rebellion spread all the way to Alabama. In North Carolina, false reports of slaves marching down the street in mobs, setting fires, and killing whites spread quickly. For two weeks after the rebellion, Black people were attacked by whites in multiple states.

Many Black people were slaughtered without a trial. In North Carolina, they killed 40 people within 24 hours. A general had to order soldiers and citizens to stop the violence, but white mobs continued looting and taking gold, jewelry, and money from dead bodies.

As for Nat Turner, he managed to escape retribution for six weeks before he was captured near his plantation. Authorities claimed he confessed to everything, but many say that was a lie. During the trial, they asked if he regretted what he did. He replied, "Was Christ not crucified?" After being hung, Nat was decapitated, and they placed his head on a spike for all to see. Many whites tried to understand why and how Nat Turner led the rebellion. They often portrayed him as a brute who only led a rebellion to get white women, not freedom.

Fearing another Nat Turner, Virginia became even stricter. Harsher slave codes forbade Negros and mulattos from learning how to read and write whether free or enslaved. Negros and mulattos were also forbidden from gathering in groups or having any religious meetings without a white person present. Anyone caught listening to a Black or white preacher at night would be whipped up to 39 times.

Many slave states passed stricter laws following Nat Turner's Rebellion. North Carolina also passed laws prohibiting free Blacks and biracial people from reading and writing. Anti- slavery literature was banned in North Carolina and many other slave states. If they caught anyone with anti-slavery pamphlets or books, they sent them to jail.

Over in Jamaica, there weren't as many whites to interfere with religious practices. Black preachers had more freedom to organize their congregation and practice religion any way they chose. Slavery on sugar plantations in Jamaica was arguably the worst. After Britain ended their participation in the slave trade, many felt slavery would be abolished altogether, but that wasn't the case. Instead of abolishing slavery, laws were passed to reduce the number of days slaves had off from three to two. They were already fed up, and that was the last straw. The tension led to an uprising known as the Christmas Rebellion or the Great Jamaican Slave Revolt.

A slave named Samuel Sharpe and many others demanded their

freedom and wanted to be paid for their work. They were only asking to be paid half of what they'd produced, but plantation owners still refused. Samuel and the others planned a peaceful strike, set to take place after Christmas when they were expected to go back to work. They agreed to only resort to violence as a last option. After the strike began, a slave owner, William Grignon, led a British militia to confront them. They tried to force the slaves back to work, but instead, Grignon was forced to retreat. Soon, the rebels took control of areas in the St. James parish.

Using guerrilla warfare tactics, they attacked British soldiers and burned down several plantations. The commander of the British soldiers, Willoughby Cotton, was forced to call in Jamaican maroons to stop the rebellion. Certain slaves were offered freedom in exchange for loyalty to the British. Maroons were often used when whites couldn't stop an uprising. But the maroons were forced to retreat as well. However, when British soldiers and the maroons began fighting together, they became too much for the insurgents.

Around 200 enslaved people were massacred, and they arrested hundreds more. The revolt only lasted two days, but it's estimated between 310 to 340 people were executed, some for offenses as small as stealing a pig. It was common for the courts to execute three or four people at a time. They shot or hung several. They killed so many Black people, bodies piled up on the street. They had to be carted out at night and buried in multiple mass grave sites outside of town.

Samuel Sharpe was accused of leading the rebellion and was the last to be executed on May 23, 1832, in Montego Bay. He was publicly lynched for all to see to send a message to others. Initially, he was labeled a criminal, but was eventually honored as the hero he was.

Today, Samuel is even on the Jamaican $50 bill. By the end of the revolt, 14 whites were killed, but over 500 Black men and women lost their lives. While the rebellion didn't immediately end slavery on the island, some say it sped up the process.

Just a few months after Nat Turner's Rebellion, the Virginia House of Delegates met for two weeks to discuss slavery. Slave breeding had become increasingly popular and extremely profitable in Virginia. Between 1790-1832, over 8,500 slaves were sold and shipped out of Virginia each year.

During the Virginia State Convention, Thomas Jefferson Randolph tried to introduce a plan for gradual emancipation, but it failed. While states like Kentucky passed laws prohibiting interstate slave trading, states like Alabama removed restrictions. Still, Black people fought for freedom in every way they could. In a court case, Menard v. Aspasia, an enslaved woman won her freedom after she was sent to Missouri from Virginia.

At the second annual Negro Convention in Philadelphia, free Blacks faced with a constant threat of being kidnapped discussed their options to leave America. They debated if they should go to Africa with the Colonization Society or leave for Canada. At the same time, a free woman named Maria W. Stewart became the first Black woman to publicly lecture against slavery. Although she didn't have any formal education, she became a teacher, a journalist, and often spoke against slavery. Inspired by David Walker, she spoke in front of mixed crowds about freedom and advocated for Africa. She even gave a speech in front of the newly formed New England Anti-Slavery Society titled "Why sit ye here and die?"

Another Black woman named Mary Prince became the first woman to write a slave narrative. She was unable to read or write, so her story had to be transcribed. It gave a firsthand account of her life as an enslaved Black woman. Mary was born as a slave in Bermuda. By the time she was 12, she was forced into hard labor, working in salt mines sometimes 17 hours a day. After being sold and separated from her family, she escaped and went back to her mother. Eventually, she made it to England as a free woman in 1828. However, Mary passed away in 1833, a year after writing her book.

By 1833, the British had passed the Slavery Abolition Act. Some say it was a response to the Jamaican slave revolt, although the law didn't end slavery. People were still forced into unpaid labor, but instead of calling it slavery, they referred to it as apprenticeships. When slaves were freed, slave owners were paid reparations for each slave they lost. The slaves who were freed were never compensated for their labor. Since Canada was still under British rule, they also adopted the Abolition Act and ended slavery in the territory.

With new hope for freedom in Canada, the Underground Railroad continued to expand.

Although Pennsylvania was a free state, laws were passed to prevent runaway slaves from passing through. In an 1833 court case, Johnson v. Tompkins, Pennsylvania strengthen the Fugitive Slave Act to discourage others from coming. The court ruled slave catchers could pursue a runaway with as much force as necessary even without proof of ownership and remove them from the state. As places like Louisiana removed restrictions on interstate slave trading, many of those taken were shipped down South.

In New York, rising tensions led to the anti-abolitionist riots, also known as the Farren Riots of 1834. When the British Parliament repealed laws that restricted emigration in Ireland, many Irish immigrants came to America. By 1835, about 30,000 Irish immigrants were arriving in New York every year. As the Irish numbers increased, so did the fighting. Although the Irish weren't considered white, they still often blamed Black people for their problems and violently attacked Black communities frequently.

The riot started after a mob of around 4,000 gathered, looking for an Englishman who had made negative comments about Americans. The mob already planned to break into a church to stop an anti-slavery meeting. However, the abolitionists didn't show up, so the group had a pro-slavery meeting instead. They mocked Black preachers and said Negros needed to be deported back to Africa, although many of them were immigrants themselves. When they couldn't find the Englishman who'd made the comments, they attacked Black neighborhoods.

The mob burned down Black businesses, homes, churches, and any building associated with Black people. They also targeted white abolitionists, burning their homes and businesses as well. The attack lasted for a little more than a week until the militia was called in. However, the violence wasn't limited to New York. In Philadelphia, the tension led to the Flying Horse Riot of 1834. The disorder started after Black and white citizens fought over seats on a merry-go- round in a building called the Flying Horse.

The next day, rumors spread that Negros had insulted whites. Soon, a horde of about a hundred gathered to attack the Flying Horse before going to the Black neighborhood. They destroyed Black taverns, homes, and two churches. The mob attacked every Black person they saw, along with anyone who tried to oppose them. Armed with clubs, bats, bricks, stones, and whatever they could find, the crowd said they were going to hunt and attack the "niggers." The riot only lasted two or three days officially, but the fighting continued. At least one Black person was killed, but they injured many more. The group looted 37 homes and destroyed at least 30, leaving many people homeless.

In Ohio, by the 1830s, there was a growing biracial population due to a rise in interracial marriages and white males raping Black women. Although Ohio was a free state, Negros and mulattos could not access public schools. However, the Ohio supreme court ruled mulattos shouldn't be denied education based on race, but anyone with majority white blood shouldn't be subject to the disability of being Black.

In a different case, the court also ruled that race would be determined by blood alone and not by sight. Anyone with 50 percent or more white blood would enjoy the same rights and privileges as whites. However, that changed in 1859 when the requirement for having a lighter complexion was added. Still, this ruling applied to civil rights questions such as voting, jury duty, and testifying in court.

By 1835, Alabama and Mississippi were producing 85 million pounds of cotton per year. Yet in the North, many anti-slavery organizations were created. In New York, the Committee of Vigilance was created to protect Black people from being kidnapped by slave catchers. Although free Blacks in North Carolina technically had the right to vote, the state passed legislation to officially disenfranchise Black residents. North Carolina also made a formal request for other states to suppress anti-slavery and abolitionist movements. South Carolina followed suit, also asking other states to suppress anything anti-slavery related.

Literature against slavery was illegal and carried harsh penalties. A white abolitionist, Amos Dresser, was publicly whipped for distributing such literature. In Boston, a mob went to William Lloyd Garrison's home and set up gallows outside of his house and threatened to lynch him. Garrison escaped and was taken to jail for his protection. Eventually, Andrew Jackson passed laws to prohibit anti-slavery literature from being sent through the mail.

Meanwhile, in 1835, Texas petitioned Mexico for statehood but was rejected. Mexico had been offering white Americans land grants, but in exchange, they'd have to speak Spanish, convert to Catholicism, and be loyal to the Mexican government. However, many slave owners didn't abide by the agreement. They refused to speak Spanish and remained Protestant. They also brought slaves into the territory against Mexican law.

Mexico passed laws to restrict white immigration into Texas. The president even repealed the Mexican Constitution of 1824 and took away the rights of states, essentially becoming a dictator. Still, white illegal immigrants continued to sneak into Mexico, but refused to follow Mexican law or pay taxes to the government. After Antonio Lopez de Santa Anna centralized the Mexican government, American colonists were angry and attempted their own uprising, known as the Texas Revolution.

Although native Tejanos were outnumbered and discriminated against by the colonists, they still fought with them against Santa Anna. However, Santa Anna quickly and violently suppressed their rebellion. For two, days Santa Anna allowed troops to pillage Texas and kill more than 2,000 people. When the attack was over, Mexican troops were sent to retrieve a cannon they'd left behind. However, the colonists refused to give it back and told them to come and take it. Santa Anna sent additional troops to take it by force, but the Texans pushed them back. For a while, they took complete control over Central Texas.

Eventually, Mexico sent reinforcements to take the land back. They caught the colonists off guard and forced them to hide in the Alamo. The Mexican army eventually killed everyone inside except for one person. They allowed slaves and some women and children to leave, but they regained control of the area, which eventually became San Antonio. This is where the saying "Remember the Alamo" came from.

Despite Mexico's objection, Texas still declared its independence, and even drafted a Declaration of Independence. Eventually, a guy named Sam Houston was elected to command the Texas army. He called for reinforcements from America, but Andrew Jackson declared neutrality. Jackson wanted to buy Mexico, not fight a war for it. Santa Anna was ruthless with anyone who opposed his rule and anything he thought would lead to a rebellion.

Santa Anna was winning the war until he decided to split up his army to search out and kill or arrest every rebel. Sam Houston caught them off guard with some help from the Tejanos. He led around 800 or 900 troops into battle with the cry "Remember the Alamo." In 18 minutes of battle, over 600 Mexicans were killed, and another 730 were captured. Only six to nine white Texans were killed.

They eventually captured Santa Anna. To get safe passage back to Mexico, he was forced to sign the Treaty of Velasco in 1836. Santa Anna agreed to end hostilities and never take up arms against Texas again. Every Mexican soldier was ordered to leave and forced back below the Rio Grande. As they left, they gave back any land or property that was taken. Finally, Santa Anna had to recognize Texas's independence and create another treaty for commerce.

Texas finally had its independence and was recognized as its own nation. Sam Houston was elected as the first official president. Texas wanted to get acceptance from America, but they were denied statehood for another ten years. Without America's help, Mexico didn't respect the treaty or recognize Texas as a nation. Although the revolution was officially over, the fighting continued. The native Tejanos also tried to join the fight against Mexico, but white colonists no longer wanted their help. Texas refused to ratify the treaties Sam Houston signed with the Cherokees, despite helping them fight for independence.

Soon, anti-Mexican rhetoric became the norm. White Texans threatened to banish or imprison every Tejano. A Tejano man named Juan Seguin was still able to become the first and only Tejano senator in Texas. He was also the only one to be elected mayor of San Antonio until 1981. However, he had to flee after white Texans accused him of supporting Mexico. Texas forced Mexico to respect the Rio Grande River as the border of Texas. Most of the Tejano population, despite siding with white Texans, were forced off their land and faced some of the discrimination Black people had been facing.

Although Texas was its own country, for Black people, it was considered a slave state. The Texas Constitution forbade free Blacks from moving or even passing through the territory. With many of the same slave codes, enslaved people could only be freed by a Congressional order. However, if freed, they had to leave the state immediately or face re-enslavement. Women also lost their rights and could no longer act or be responsible for themselves.

To whites, they saw the rebellion in Texas as a revolution, although they were the ones who broke their agreement. Yet, when it came to Nat Turner's revolution, they labeled it as just a rebellion, although he was fighting for freedom. But as the age-old saying goes, "Those who control the media, control the narrative."

CHAPTER 12.
THE SECOND SEMINOLE WAR:
A TRAIL OF TEARS

In keeping with tradition, when Europeans want something, they take it by force. After gold was discovered in Georgia, Andrew Jackson planned to take the land. Many tribes were forced to sign treaties to give up their region. Some tribes refused, but Jackson was ready to take it by force.

After signing the Treaty of Payne's Landing in 1834, they were given three years to move west of the Mississippi River. America claimed the agreement began two years earlier, so tribes only had a year to leave. Many native leaders denied signing the treaty at all, while others were forced to sign it. Jackson sent a letter threatening to use the militia to remove any tribes who refused to leave. Still, many stayed.

Tensions rose until whites began attacking Indigenous people. Although the term "Seminole" is often synonymous with Indians, originally, it was used to refer to runaway slaves. Many of the heroes in the Seminole Wars were Black. Since many Black Seminoles spoke English, they often acted as translators between the Seminoles and the Americans. A runaway slave named John Caeser organized and led attacks on several plantations. Eventually, 200 others he'd helped free joined him. In a battle known as the Dade massacre, another former slave named John Horse used guerrilla warfare tactics to attack U.S troops. The rebels, led by Horse, pushed U.S. troops back, and only three soldiers survived.

After the battle, Andrew Jackson called in volunteers from Florida, Georgia, and South Carolina for reinforcement. Nearly 1,100 troops were sent to Florida. Still, John Horse and John Caeser led many successful battles against them. As they attacked U.S. forts, including Fort Alabama, they also burned down plantations along the way. After being defeated time and time again, Andrew Jackson appointed Thomas Jesup as commander of the U.S. military.

Jesup had just suppressed an uprising in the Creek War of 1836. He'd forced the Creek tribe to sign the Treaty of Cusseta and had them either sell their land and move west or become citizens, subject to state laws and taxes. Jesup planned to wear down the Seminoles over time instead of continuing to send large numbers of troops. Although he was known as the "Father of the Quartermaster Corps," he had to use deception to beat the Seminoles.

Jesup was in command of nearly 9,000 soldiers, but still resorted to lying about a truce to capture Seminole leaders. In 1836, he wrote a letter to the Secretary of War saying, "This, you may be assured, is a Negro, not an Indian War." He added, "If it be not speedily put down, the south will feel the effects of it on their slave population before the end of the next season." The Secretary of War replied, "You will allow no terms to the Indians until every living slave in their possession belonging to a white man is given up."

Soon Virginia, Georgia, and Alabama joined the Carolinas in requesting other states to suppress any anti-slavery activity. Congress ended up issuing a gag rule to postpone action on every petition to end slavery. Even white abolitionists received more backlash than before. A white guy in Georgia named Aaron W. Kitchell was tarred and feathered by a mob after being accused of inciting Negros. In Ohio and Vermont, insurgents attacked abolitionist newspaper offices to stop them from publishing.

After Arkansas was officially admitted into the union as the 25th state, it became the 13th state to legalize slavery. As things were slowly changing in the North, a Massachusetts law declared that any slave brought into the state by an owner would be freed. However, like every free state, the Fugitive Slave Law was still in effect. Whether free, enslaved, or a runaway, Black men, women, and children were in constant danger, even in free states.

An enslaved woman named Harriet Ann Jacobs managed to escape and eventually became an anti-slavery activist. Harriet was born in North Carolina, enslaved by cruel owners. Although she learned how to read and write, her enslavers constantly raped her as a child. When she got older and wanted to get married, the owner wouldn't allow it. Harriet started dating white men and even had children with them, hoping it'd lead to freedom. Still, the owner refused to let her go. He threatened to sell her children if she refused to have sex with him, although she did everything she could to avoid him.

By 1835, it was so bad for Harriett she chose to hide in a crawl space in her grandmother's house for seven years to escape. Eventually, she made it to Philadelphia en route to New York. Harriett was forced to leave her children behind, although she eventually reunited with her daughter in New York. Harriet Jacobs went on to become an anti-slavery speaker and author. In 1861, she published an autobiography, Incidents in the Life of a Slave Girl. It was one of the first books highlighting freedom and the sexual abuse of Black women. It also highlighted Black women's roles as women and mothers.

In 1836, a Black woman named Henrietta Ray, who was also an anti-slavery activist, passed away at 28. Henrietta helped create a community aid society for Black women called the African Dorcas Association. The organization also sewed clothes for Black children to attend the African Free School. Henrietta was also the owner and editor of the Colored American newspaper. A few years before she passed, she was elected president of the New York Female Literary Society.

Meanwhile, by 1835, Europeans in South Africa moved further inland in what was known as the "Great Trek." Britain had already colonized Cape Town by 1814, leading to mass migration. With different groups in the area, including Dutch farmers or Boers, Britain wanted to "Britainize" the area to maintain control. They passed policies to give themselves an advantage over other groups. For example, English was made the official language, although the Boers weren't fluent.

The British also strongly opposed them owning slaves, feeling they were too harsh. In 1828, the governor of Cape Town declared all native inhabitants, except slaves, would have equal rights as citizens. But the Dutch weren't the only ones affected. Every European group in the area, including British residents, was furious. Still, Britain created political and judicial systems favoring English-speaking whites in the area. Once

Britain officially abolished slavery in 1834, many Europeans saw it as the last straw, especially the Boers. At least 94 percent of the Dutch farmers in the area owned and depended on slave labor.

In the first wave, more than 6,000 made the trek, over 20 percent of the population. As they encroached on native lands, they had many run-ins with local tribes, including the Zulu nation. Most tribes refused to back down, instead choosing to protect themselves from white invaders by fighting back. A few tribes surrendered their land, fearing their people would be slaughtered by European weapons. However, the expanded Zulu nation was one of the tribes who refused to comply.

In one battle, the Zulu army killed 282 Boers, including 185 children, 56 women, and 41 men. They fought constantly until it culminated with the Battle of Blood River. In that battle, about 480 Boers surrounded a Zulu army of about 12,000. The problem for the Zulu army was they were only armed with spears. They didn't have a chance against Europeans who were armed with guns. Nearly 3,000 Zulu warriors were killed. Since no whites were killed, they saw it as a sign from God to destroy the natives, kill them off, and take their land.

The Dutch also instigated civil wars in the Zulu nation over control. By 1838, they established the first white independent free state in the area called Fort Natal. But by 1843, the British took back control of the land. They didn't recognize the Boers' independence until 1854, and they are still there today. Throughout the twentieth century, the Boers were one of the main groups responsible for creating the apartheid system in South Africa. It took until 2013 for Julius Malema and the EFF to demand the land back.

While the "Great Trek" was taking place in South Africa, there was also a mass migration taking place in America. Early in 1837, the war took a turn for the worse for the Seminoles. They were increasingly being killed or captured in battle. In the Battle of Hatchee- Lustee Creek, 30 or 40 men, women, and children were captured. Some Seminole chiefs signed treaties and agreed to move West. Before they could leave, slave catchers claimed many of the Seminoles as property, often winning disputes because there was no written record. Others were accused by whites of owing debts or committing crimes and were arrested.

Although some tribes surrendered, many knew Europeans wouldn't uphold a treaty.

They knew they had to fight. By June, about 200 men planned to break into detention camps to free 700 Seminoles who had been captured. Jesup didn't plan on a long battle and felt the war was over. Many of his troops were relocated, and most of the volunteers were released from duty. He was running out of resources, but the fight wasn't over.

Congress approved another $1.6 million for the war, but Jesup still resorted to deception.

He requested meetings with the remaining Seminole leaders. He pretended to wave the white flag, then captured them under false pretenses. Some of those who were captured, including John Horse, escaped. Even though the U.S. barely had enough resources to feed their troops, the Seminoles continued taking losses, and many surrendered. During the Battle of Lake Okeechobee, only a few Seminoles were killed, but they were still pushed back. The U.S. saw it as a great victory, despite having more casualties.

By 1837, America was producing 500 million pounds of cotton per year, with over 2 million slaves on record. Still, an economic panic led to many of the early white labor unions collapsing. That year, Michigan entered the union as the 26th state and a free territory. At the same time, the U.S. House of Representatives ruled slaves had no right to petition Congress for freedom or any reason. Congress also passed stricter gag rule laws to eradicate anti-slavery propaganda. A publisher of an anti-slavery newspaper named Elijah Lovejoy was killed by a mob in Illinois.

By 1837, 10,000 former enslaved people were living in Upper Canada. Meanwhile, in New York, the first Black publication, the Weekly Advocate, circulated in free Black communities. The publication was later changed to the Colored American. But free Black men in New York still had to petition just to keep their voting rights. Pennsylvania and Mississippi also limited voting to certain white males only. Fearing retribution, states continued to pass laws to discourage any ideas of an uprising.

Texas instituted laws to increase the punishment to death for raping (looking) at a white woman. It was also punishable by death if a slave was caught poisoning, injuring, or assaulting a white person. Additionally, burglary, arson, and murder were punishable by death. If a Negro, free or enslaved, was accused of planning a revolt, it meant automatic death. In Louisiana, in 1837, an enslaved man named Lewis Cheney planned an uprising known as the Cheneyville Conspiracy.

Lewis was furious after being demoted from a house slave to a field slave. He organized both free and enslaved Negros, and a few whites, to fight. He organized close to 50 slaves on five plantations. However, before the uprising began, Lewis told his owner about the plan. In exchange, he was freed and given $500 so he could leave the state, although it was his idea. His owner was given $1000 as compensation for losing a slave.

Whites didn't realize how serious the plan was until they heard Black people were debating if they should kill children or not. Many people suspected of being involved were forced to confess on the gallows. Nine enslaved people and three free Blacks were sentenced to death by hanging. State officials didn't want word to get out, so they suppressed it as much as possible. But in the Black community, the name Lewis Cheney was despised and became synonymous with a traitor or sellout.

Despite numerous attempted petitions to abolish slavery by free Blacks, they were repeatedly denied by Congress. However, Congress accepted a presentation from a South Carolina senator named John Calhoun. Congress approved his proposal to protect the institution of slavery and to resist efforts by free states to use the issue of slavery to get laws passed for other domestic issues.

With America strengthening the institution of slavery, by 1838, new routes on the Underground Railroad were established. A slave named Frederick Bailey managed to get to Philadelphia from Maryland. After escaping slavery, he changed his name to Frederick Douglass. One of his friends, David Ruggles, is said to have led more than 600 slaves to freedom, including Frederick. David Ruggles is generally known as the first Black bookseller in America after opening his own store in 1834. Although a white mob destroyed his store, David continued to publish anti-slavery and pro-Black literature. Also, Phillis Wheatley's book, Memoirs and Poems of Phillis Wheatley, A Native African and a Slave, was published in Boston.

Meanwhile, in Florida, the Second Seminole War continued with the Battle of Loxahatchee. When U.S. soldiers came across a group of Seminoles, they were forced to retreat. Jesup sent 1,500 more soldiers for reinforcement to defeat them. Many Seminole warriors were captured and gave little resistance once they were detained. But Jesup was unwilling to let 500 prisoners go.

In Georgia, around 2,000 members of the Cherokee tribe voluntarily left their land for Oklahoma. Many more were forced to leave, however, and close to 4,000 died during the journey. After one last treaty, Andrew Jackson took the remaining land. He forced about 13,000 from the Cherokee tribe to migrate to Cleveland and Tennessee. The 1,000-mile trek began during the winter. They weren't allowed to go into any towns, which made the journey longer. When they attempted to cross a river, they were forced to pay a dollar per person for a toll that was normally 12 cents. They were also forced to wait for every white person to cross the bridge first.

Many of the Cherokee died waiting to cross, huddled together at Mantle Rock. Some were also murdered by local whites. The Cherokee sued the American government to pay for the burial of their loved ones killed during the journey. America weakened the Cherokees, who also owned Black slaves, by killing their food supply. Then using deception, they pretended to make a peace offering by giving them blankets infected with smallpox. However, some say evidence shows they used blankets with smallpox during the French and Indian War, not the Trail of Tears.

As people were forced to walk across America, a Spanish slave ship called the Amistad was transporting 53 kidnapped Africans, including 4 children, to Cuba. During the voyage, an enslaved man named Joseph Cinque or Sengbe Pieh led a revolt to take over the ship. Many of them had already heard rumors their captors were planning to kill and eat them. Somehow, they broke out of their chains and used machetes to kill the ship's captain and most of the crew. They kept some of the crew alive and ordered them to turn the ship around to go back to Africa. Of course, they lied and took them to America.

They eventually arrived in Long Island, NY, where the rebels were arrested. They were taken to Connecticut to be held until trial. Although

Spain had already banned the slave trade and Cuba had outlawed slavery, the governor still allowed slave trading if he was given money for each slave who was brought into the colony. Since importing slaves was illegal, the ship's owner lied. He claimed the slaves were born in Cuba and were being sold in the Spanish domestic slave trade to avoid trouble. Although two other Spaniards were also illegally captured, they were released while the Africans were put in jail.

The Spanish wanted Joseph and the others placed on trial for mutiny, piracy, and murder. Martin Van Buren, who became president in 1837, initially agreed and was in favor of sending them to Cuba to be tried. However, the rebels who took over the Amistad were seen as an inspiration to many, even white abolitionists. Some white Americans argued since the slave trade was illegal, the rebels acted in self-defense, including John Quincy Adams, who defended them in court.

When the trial started in 1840, Van Buren had Joseph and the others shipped to Cuba in case they were found guilty. The judge in the trial ruled the rebels on the Amistad were kidnapping victims. He said they were free Negros of Africa that were falsely sold as slaves.

The judge also ruled they be set free and transported back to their homeland. Van Buren tried to appeal the decision, arguing the verdict would encourage others to fight back. He did everything he could to keep them enslaved and send them to Cuba, even appealing to the Supreme Court.

During the trial, a 10-year-old boy who was taken on the Amistad learned enough English to write a letter that was leaked in newspapers. He wrote, "We don't want to go to Havana. All we want is make us free." After years of waiting, in 1841, the Supreme Court upheld the ruling to free them in a vote of seven to one. But with no money, they were forced to stay in Connecticut until they raised enough to get back home. Eventually, they were able to return home in 1842, but by then, the effects of colonization had changed everything.

When the Amistad had first arrived in America in 1839, Ohio had just passed another Fugitive Slave Act. Many whites, mostly Irish immigrants, were angry people were escaping slavery and coming into the state. The act was also passed for slave owners in surrounding states, especially

Kentucky. The sixth Census in 1840 showed close to 2.5 million people were enslaved in the U.S. Only 386,300 Negros were considered free. Due to all the Fugitive Slave Laws, New York finally passed a law to protect free Black citizens from being kidnapped. Free Black men, women, and especially children, were being kidnapped so much, New York had to address the problem. A movie like 12 Years a Slave gave a little insight into how dangerous it was for free Negros, although the reality was much worse.

In South Carolina, more Black Codes were passed, and others were reinforced. Black people, free or enslaved, were forbidden from gathering in groups, earning money, growing their own food, carrying weapons, and learning how to read and write. They even passed laws to forbid Black people from owning or wearing high-quality, nice clothing. Although it applied to every Negro, the law was directed at Black women. They weren't allowed to dress nice, upkeep their hair, wear makeup, or do anything to make themselves more attractive. White women were especially jealous because a lot of white males still preferred enslaved Black women over them.

Since Texas was its own country, they passed their own slave codes. Enslaved people were forbidden from trading, buying, or selling goods without permission. Free and enslaved Negros were also forbidden from carrying any kind of weapon without written permission. But in Florida, the Seminole warriors refused to give up and fought back any way they could.

The war had been going on for almost four years and was costing the U.S. a lot of money. Van Buren decided to send a general to Florida to create a new treaty. However, knowing Europeans rarely keep their treaties, the Seminoles were slow to respond. When they responded, they made an offer to stop fighting in exchange for land. The U.S. imported bloodhounds from Cuba to hunt the Seminoles down, but since they were in swampy areas, bringing in dogs wasn't effective.

The Seminoles continued to attack U.S. troops, often catching them by surprise. Using the land to their advantage, they made it difficult for the Americans to retaliate. U.S. soldiers resorted to burning their fields, destroying their food, killing their livestock, and even killing their horses.

As the war continued, battles were decided by whichever side was able to catch the other off guard. Since most of the Black Seminoles were runaway slaves, they knew how often treaties and promises were broken. They refused to go back into slavery and chose to fight to keep their freedom, even if it meant death.

CHAPTER 13.
MANIFEST DESTINY: THE DRED SCOTT DECISION

In 1841, Frederick Douglass gave his first speech about abolishing slavery to an all- white audience. We often talk to other audiences when we could be talking to ourselves. Not long after Frederick gave his speech, an anti-slavery newspaper reported he was racially profiled and kicked off a train. Things were getting so bad for free Negros, Ohio reinstituted laws to deter whites from kidnapping Black people.

Many poor whites, especially immigrants like the Irish, tried to make money by selling free Negros into slavery. They often blamed their problems on Black people and were increasingly violent since the riot of 1829. Lynch mobs even attacked white abolitionists who they referred to as "nigger lovers." They burned printing presses for anti-slavery newspapers and attacked and murdered several Black men. These problems weren't only in Ohio. In DC, a free man named Solomon Northup was kidnapped and sold into slavery for 12 years. He went on to write the book 12 Years a Slave about his experience, which the movie was based on.

Meanwhile, in Illinois, Abraham Lincoln won a court case to free a young Black girl. In Bailey v. Cromwell, Lincoln argued the Northwest Ordinance of 1787 outlawed slavery in the state. The court agreed that selling the enslaved girl was illegal. Essentially, it meant all Black people in Illinois were free, in theory. Although Illinois was technically a free state, Texas was still acting as its own nation. They reinforced laws against slaves, especially runaways. White citizens not only had the right to catch runaways and turn them in to the police, it was their responsibility. If a slave couldn't be returned to their plantation, they were put on the auction block to be sold.

In Rhode Island, 60 percent of the white population still couldn't vote in 1841. Many white immigrants, mainly the Irish, didn't own land, which was a requirement to vote. When a white guy named Thomas Dorr led a movement to expand voting rights, Irish immigrants excluded Black people. The Dorr Rebellion failed miserably after adding a whites-only clause.

Dorr led his followers to take over the city's arsenal, but it was guarded by some of his family members. When the guards refused to surrender, he tried to fire a cannon; but it didn't work. He became a laughingstock and was eventually arrested. He was the first to be convicted of treason against the state. Dorr wasn't lynched or punished; in fact, he was out of jail by 1845.

The same year, the Amistad victims were exonerated, a man named Madison Washington led one of the most successful slave revolts. Madison was born enslaved in Virginia but managed to escape to Canada. However, his wife was still enslaved, and he realized it would take too long to buy her freedom. He felt his freedom was nothing without his wife, so he decided to return to Virginia to save her. Since she was unable to escape with him, he stayed in Virginia to be near her.

Eventually, Madison returned to Canada, determined to free his wife. With the money he earned, he bought weapons and concealed them in his clothing. Since he was still wanted, he hid his identity and traveled at night to avoid being recognized. Madison ended up stumbling across a corn shucking, where slaves were rewarded for peeling large amounts of corn with a feast and whiskey. After being stripped of everything, they found any reason to uplift their spirits, so they often sang and danced during a corn shucking.

Madison blended in and asked a few questions but didn't eat any food for fear of being recognized. He found out where his wife was, but he was so anxious to see her he was spotted by an overseer. The first three white guys who approached him were knocked unconscious.

Eventually, enough backup arrived to subdue Madison. He was shipped to Richmond, VA to be sold in the epicenter of interstate slave trading in America.

Madison was sold to Johnson and Epperson and was set to be shipped to New Orleans. He and 144 others were heavily shackled and placed on a ship called the Creole. Knowing he still had weapons in the lining of his clothes, Madison cooperated as he was chained to the floor. The conditions on these ships were no different from any other slave ship, with men held in one cabin and the women and children in another.

On the ninth day of the trip, Madison finally saw the right opportunity to strike. Using a saw and other weapons he had concealed, he was able to break free. He freed 18 others who he thought would help, and they attacked the ship's crew, catching them by surprise. They wanted to kill them all, but Madison wouldn't allow it. He even got the crew members medical treatment. Once they healed, they tried to regain control of the ship but failed. Madison was named captain of the ship, and he ordered the chef to prepare a feast to celebrate their freedom.

Although he wanted to go to Sierra Leone, it was too far. He ordered the surviving crew members to take them to the Bahamas where slavery was outlawed. One hundred and sixteen people were freed as soon as they landed. Five of them chose to stay on board and return to slavery in New Orleans. When the ship arrived with only five people, their enslavers were infuriated. They demanded that Madison and the others be returned. However, since slavery was outlawed and there was no extradition or treaties between Britain and America, they remained free.

Madison Washington and the men who helped him fight were arrested. However, in 1842, the court ordered they be released as free men. Madison freed himself from slavery twice, after risking it all to free his wife. The second time, he was able to free over 130 others, including his wife. There's a reason we know about the Amistad case, and there's even a movie about it. But we rarely hear about the Creole case. The victims on the Amistad had to ask, "Give us, us free." But in Madison's case, he took freedom and led one of the most successful slave revolts. Even though his previous plans failed, this true hero and warrior didn't give up and helped free many others without knowing his wife was on board the Creole.

Not long after the Creole case, a ruling in another court case deemed the federal government responsible for slave catching. The case Prigg v. Pennsylvania essentially created federal agents out of slave catchers. It began when a slave catcher named Edward Prigg kidnapped a Black woman named Margaret Morgan and her daughter. After Pennsylvania passed laws against kidnapping and selling free Blacks into slavery, it was more difficult to take runaways out of Pennsylvania than anywhere else.

Prigg followed procedure but didn't have enough evidence to remove Margaret and her children from the state. After he was denied, he took them to Maryland against their will anyway. Prigg was arrested, charged, and convicted under the anti-kidnapping statute. He appealed to the Supreme Court, arguing the state's right to protect free Negros didn't supersede the Fugitive Slave Act. The court ruled federal law overruled state law, and Prigg's conviction was overturned. The court also ruled slave catching was the responsibility of the government, and they could no longer force white citizens to be on slave patrols if they didn't want to.

Whether the slave patrol was federal or not, it didn't matter to slaves trying to escape. In 1842, a free man named William Wells Brown led a group of 69 runaway slaves to Canada.

William had already escaped slavery and used his experience working on steamboats to help others. Some felt leaving America was their only hope. In Rhode Island, voting rights were extended to any native-born male, including Black men, if they met the age limit. However, poll taxes prevented many Negros from voting. Rhode Island also excluded the Narragansett tribe because they were darker-skinned people.

Down South, Georgia unanimously passed legislation to declare free Blacks were not citizens of America. Many states, especially free states, focused on protecting the personal liberty of white citizens. In states like Ohio, New York, and Vermont, whites were no longer persecuted if they didn't join the slave patrol, although it was still illegal to give slaves refuge. Inspired to make a change, Sojourner Truth escaped slavery in New York. She changed her name and became the first Black woman to join the anti-slavery lecture circuit.

Meanwhile, in Indiana, Frederick Douglass was beaten by a white mob. White crowds felt violence would deter abolitionists, especially Black ones. But they refused to back down. At the National Negro Convention in Buffalo, NY, Henry Highland Garnet gave his most famous speech, A Call to Rebellion. He suggested, instead of trying to convince or sway whites to grow a heart and end slavery, Black people should take their freedom by rising against slave owners.

Henry also said, "Neither God nor angels, or just men command you suffer for a single moment; therefore, it is your duty to use every means, both moral, intellectual, and physical that promise success." Although he was referring to a boycott and not necessarily killing, many, including Frederick Douglass, saw it as extreme. Frederick spoke out against Henry's speech and condemned it at the meeting. Henry responded, but he was eventually voted against. Henry favored the idea of leaving America, and he eventually moved to Jamaica. There, he continued to fight against the system and preached about establishing separate sections in different nations for Black people.

Meanwhile, in 1844, James Polk was elected as the 11th president of America, and was the 9th to own slaves. Polk became a slave owner as a child, and even purchased several slaves, including children, while in office. As president, Polk pushed the idea of "manifest destiny," a term coined in 1845. They believed America was destined by God to spread its dominion across the entire continent. They felt God had given them the right to take the land and enslave the people.

Congress also lifted the gag rule set in place to stop petitions on abolishing slavery. States like Connecticut continued to pass personal liberty laws to protect white citizens who didn't want to participate in the slave patrol. Oregon decided to outlaw slavery in the state completely. However, North Carolina completely denied citizenship to all Negros in 1844.

Many free Negros were forced to leave the state; some were even enslaved.

As the issue of slavery became more complicated, the Underground Railroad continued to grow as more people tried to escape. A free Black man named William Still helped as many people as he could reach freedom. In Florida, a white abolitionist named Jonathan Walker helped several slaves escape to the West Indies where slavery was illegal. Walker was ultimately arrested and convicted. He was sentenced to be tied to a pillar and publicly branded as a slave stealer. But since Walker was white, he wasn't executed or treated the same as a Black abolitionist.

In 1845, Texas was finally admitted into the Union as a slave state after repeated attempts. Although manifest destiny was an American concept, the same thing was taking place globally. The British convinced leaders of the Fante people to sign the Bond of 1844. At least eight chiefs signed the Bond, giving the British control of the land. Some saw signing the agreement as signing away their sovereignty to foreign powers. But the Fante people felt it was better to be controlled by the British than the Asante empire.

The British didn't respect the Asante culture and wanted access to the land. They took advantage of tribal issues and formed an alliance with the Fante people in order to do so. Dating back to 1806, conflicts with the expanding Asante empire led to the first Asante-Fante War. The British used their war to gain access to the land and capitalized as both sides exchanged captured prisoners for guns and other goods.

The Akan people who were sold into slavery were known as the Coromantee. The Coromantee led many revolts and caused fear in Europeans. It was one of the factors that played into the slave trade being banned. The Akan people used indentured servants themselves to clear land, but it wasn't close to the chattel slavery Europeans practiced. Still, as Europeans expanded the Gold Coast settlement, the Asante and Akan tribes traded indentured servants and prisoners of war to the British. In 2006, Ghana apologized to the descendants of the slave trade for the role they played. The Asante tribe fought as well and defeated the colonizers on some occasions, including in the Anglo-Asante wars.

Meanwhile, in South Africa, Britain declared control over Natal. They also gained control over Zululand after the Zulu king, Dingane, died in 1840. Although the land was given to the Boers, the natives continued to fight back. As the French continued to expand on the Gold Coast, they built more slave forts, including the forts of Assinie, Bassam, and Dabou. The French got the chiefs of local tribes to sign treaties, which allowed them to make the area a permanent trading center.

Back in America, free Blacks citizens in New England created the Freedom Association to aid runaway slaves in 1845. That year, a man named Macon Bolling Allen became the first Black person to pass the bar and practice law in Massachusetts. In entertainment, a Black man named William Henry Lane, aka Master Juba, was considered the first famous

Black performer in America. He was one of the first Black people to join the minstrel shows. William wore blackface and made fun of himself in front of an all-white audience. Although Black entertainers were paid, they weren't even allowed in the building unless they were performing. Even then, they still had to use the back entrance.

After Florida and Texas were finally admitted into the Union as slave states, a columnist named John O'Sullivan helped Polk coin the term "manifest destiny." It didn't matter that people already lived on the land, America felt it all belonged to them, "from sea to shining sea."

To take California, Polk invaded Mexico after they refused to give up their land. Before Congress declared war, the U.S. offered Mexico $30 million to buy New Mexico and California.

However, Mexico was still upset Texas was a part of America. They didn't have enough resources or manpower to stop the U.S. from taking what they wanted, so, eventually, Mexico signed the Treaty of Guadalupe Hidalgo in 1848. The treaty ended the war with the U.S., but Mexico ceded nearly 55 percent of its land. America received California, Arizona, Nevada, Utah, and parts of New Mexico, Wyoming, and Colorado in exchange for $15 million, plus another $5 million to pay the claims of American citizens. Mexican citizens in those territories were only left with the option of leaving or becoming American citizens, subject to laws and taxes.

The Treaty of Guadalupe Hidalgo alone helped expand the idea of manifest destiny. Onc U.S. representative wanted to push the Wilmot Proviso to ban slavery in the newly acquired territories. However, the Senate rejected it. Instead, Texas's state legislature created a formal slave patrol system. Thcsc slave catchers, also known as patty rollers, eventually grew into the modern-day police. The first slave patrol was established in 1704 in South Carolina, but by the 1840s, it reached another level.

Meanwhile, in St. Louis, MI, a Black man named Moses Dickson founded the Knights of Liberty in 1846. The Knights of Liberty was a secret organization that planned to organize a national uprising to end slavery. The plan was to recruit slaves from the South and train them to prepare for an attack within 10 years. Within those 10 years, the organization grew from 12 men to nearly 42,000, with people in every state except Texas and Mississippi. Although they were fighting for their liberation, Moses still ordered them to spare the women and children and to treat their prisoners well.

Moses and the others expected over 200,000 people to join them by the time they reached Atlanta. But after setting a date for the uprising, it was called off because people expected the Civil War to happen at any time. Still, the organization became a part of the Underground Railroad and helped many escape slavery. Although New York passed more laws to abolish slavery in 1846, Missouri repealed the laws against interstate slave trading. The next year, Missouri even passed laws to forbid free Negros from reading, writing, or getting an education.

Over in Africa, Tunisia officially abolished slavery in 1847. Slavery in Tunisia dated back to the Trans-Saharan slave trade, way before the Atlantic slave trade. That year, Liberia declared itself an independent nation and became the first democratic republic in Africa since colonization. They created their own Constitution, although they received approval from America. A Black man from Virginia named Joseph Jenkins was elected as the first president of Liberia. Elsewhere, Sweden abolished slavery in 1847.

Back in America, Pennsylvania finally began enforcing the anti-kidnapping personal liberty laws for free Blacks. The U.S. House of Representatives also passed the Oregon Bill. The bill outlawed slavery in Oregon so Texas could remain a slave state. Still, despite the odds in Chicago, David Jones Peck became the first Black person to graduate from a medical school in America. Another Black man named Robert Morris Sr. became the first Black lawyer to file a lawsuit, and he won. Robert also was the first to challenge segregated public schools in Roberts v. Boston in 1848. It was considered the first legal challenge of "separate but equal," although the Supreme Court ruled against him in 1850.

As Robert challenged segregation, a slave named Dred Scott was challenging the system in his own way. Dred was born enslaved in Virginia and was moved to Alabama before being sent to Missouri. After his enslaver died, he was purchased by John Emerson, who moved him to Illinois before taking him to Wisconsin. There, he met an enslaved woman named Harriet Robinson and married her. Since Illinois and Wisconsin were free territories, Dred had the right to make a legal claim for freedom, although he never did.

Eventually, Emerson moved back down South, and Dred was sent back to Missouri. After Emerson died, his wife Irene Emerson leased Dred until he learned about his right to claim freedom. He offered to buy his freedom, along with his family's, but Emerson refused his offer. Using the doctrine of "once free, always free," Dred and his wife filed freedom lawsuits. A Missouri law passed in 1824 said slaves were to be freed after living in a free state for a certain period of time, and would remain free even if taken back to Missouri. Despite having legal standing, Dred and his wife were denied freedom by the courts.

The court claimed since he couldn't prove they were owned by Irene Emerson, he couldn't sue for freedom. Dred was granted a retrial, but it was delayed until 1850. During the retrial, he and his family were granted freedom. But two years later, the Missouri Supreme Court stepped in and overturned the decision. Left with no choice, Dred took his case to the

U.S. Supreme Court. However, seven of nine justices on the Supreme Court had been appointed by slave-owning presidents, and at least five judges came from slave-owning families.

Eventually, they ruled against him in a seven to two decision. Dred and his family were sent back to slavery. The court's opinion, read by Chief Justice Roger Taney, was that Negros were not included and were never intended to be included under the word citizens in the constitution. They said Negros couldn't claim any rights, privileges, or protections for American citizens. Using laws dating back to the Constitution, Taney said there was a "perpetual and impassable barrier" intended to be between the white race and the one they reduced to slavery.

Taney also claimed both free and enslaved Negros were beings of an "inferior order and altogether unfit to associate with the white race." He said, Negros were so inferior they had no rights which the white man was bound to respect. To this day, no law or court ruling has officially overturned the Dred Scott decision. That's why Black people still fight for the civil rights that American citizens already have. For example, the Voting Rights Act of 1965 still has to be voted on and renewed every 25 years. The Dred Scott decision also ruled that the Missouri Compromise was unconstitutional.

The court added Congress had no power to say which state could allow slavery or regulate it, but it was up to the state. The Dred Scott ruling essentially ended the debate on where Black people stood in America if there was still any question.

CHAPTER 14.
FUGITIVE SLAVE ACTS: THE GREAT ESCAPE

Unlike Dred Scott and Robert Morris Sr., not everyone attempted to get their freedom through the courts. In 1848, about 70 slaves tried to escape from slavery in Washington, DC, on a ship called The Pearl. After two days of rough weather, they were captured on the Chesapeake Bay near Point Lookout, MD. All of them were sold and shipped further down South to Georgia or Louisiana. Many were taken to the New Orleans slave market.

White residents were outraged over the attempted escape and rioted for three days. They attacked abolitionists and publishers for promoting anti-slavery propaganda. The white abolitionists who helped them escape were charged and convicted. They served four years before they were pardoned.

That year, states like Rhode Island, Vermont, Connecticut, New York, and Ohio passed more personal liberty anti-kidnapping laws. However, these laws were meant to protect white citizens from being forced to capture runaways more so than to protect free Blacks. While South Carolina was busy removing laws against interstate slave trading, gold was discovered in California. Many people moved out West, hoping to get rich.

A large number of people were caught up in the California Gold Rush, but slaves were doing anything they could to get to freedom in the North. An enslaved married couple, Ellen and William Craft escaped from slavery in Macon, GA. They arrived in Philadelphia before eventually moving to England. Ellen was the daughter of a white slave owner and an enslaved woman. Although she was still considered a slave, she was three-fourths white and noticed that she could pass as a white woman. Eventually, her father and owner allowed her to marry William, who had more freedom than other slaves.

William was often rented out but was allowed to keep most of the money he made as a carpenter. William and Ellen wanted to start a family, so they saved money and planned their escape for Christmas of 1848. Ellen knew she could use the fact she could pass as white to pose as a slave owner traveling with her slave. Since white women generally weren't allowed to travel alone, especially with a male slave, she cut her hair and dressed as a young white male.

Ellen pretended to be deaf so she wouldn't have to talk to anyone. Since she couldn't read or write, she tied her arm in a sling so she wouldn't have to sign anything. They covered her face in bandages to hide her skin, and she kept glasses on to hide her eyes. Still, William and Ellen had several close calls. They traveled first-class on trains and stayed at the nicest hotels.

They figured they'd hide in plain sight. During their journey, whites warned Ellen about being too nice to her slave and told her to make sure he didn't escape.

At one point, Ellen even sat next to a friend of her owner and father, but he didn't recognize her. During the last major stop in Baltimore, Ellen and William were detained until she showed proof of ownership for William. Maryland was the last state many slaves went through before reaching freedom, and it was heavily guarded. When the authorities refused to let them go, William said he felt they were in deep water and were being overwhelmed. But as the train was about to leave, for some reason, the authorities changed their mind and let them pass.

They made it to Philadelphia on Christmas morning after the four-day journey. Ellen and William became popular telling their story, but it led to more slave catchers trying to hunt them down. After stricter Fugitive Slave Laws were passed, William and Ellen left Boston for England. There, they had five children, all born free. Twenty years after the Civil War, they returned to America and opened a school for Black children in Georgia.

By 1848, slavery was abolished in Denmark. France had also abolished slavery in its colonies and granted full voting rights. Black cities were able to elect their own representatives. But in America, the institution of slavery was still in full effect. Although his strategy was different from

William and Ellen Craft, Henry "Box" Brown was determined to get his freedom by any means. Henry was born near Richmond, VA, and married an enslaved woman named Nancy. They had three children, but since Nancy was enslaved, so were their children.

Henry paid Nancy's enslaver so he wouldn't sell her or their children. Eventually, Henry was betrayed. After coming home from working in a tobacco factory, he discovered his wife and children had been sold. Not long after, he had the idea to mail himself to a free state. Stuffing himself into a box three feet long, three feet deep, and two feet wide, Henry cut out a small hole for air and only took a few biscuits and some water. To get out of work, he burned his hands to the bone with oil of vitriol.

Henry was transported in the box by wagon, train, steamboat, another wagon, another train, a ferry, and another train before being delivered to Philadelphia. Although the box was labeled "handle with care, this side up," the box was flipped and tossed around several times. At one point, Henry was flipped on his head for about an hour and a half. Although he almost died, Henry was able to stay quiet. After traveling for 27 hours, he finally reached freedom. Henry said it was worth the risk to get his freedom, but after the Fugitive Slave Act of 1850, he moved to England. There, he met his second wife, a white woman named Jane Floyd.

Harriet Tubman escaped slavery herself in 1849. She was one of the most famous freedom fighters and helped many enslaved people escape North. She got to Philadelphia from Maryland by herself. Within a year of gaining her freedom, Harriet got word that her sister and children were going to be sold. She said she was happy to be free, but her family deserved to be free with her. Not long after, she went back to Maryland and led her sister and her two children to freedom.

Still, Harriet wasn't done. She went back again, this time for her brother and anyone who wanted to go. The third time she went back it was for her husband, but he had already taken another wife and refused to go. She left him there but took anybody willing to go with her. Harriet went back a fourth time for her parents, and she kept returning to free as many people as she could. Eventually, she was given the nickname Moses because she led so many people to freedom.

Each time she returned, Harriet improved her techniques to stay hidden. She used codes, blankets, and songs to communicate. Harriet often left on Saturday nights because the news of missing slaves wouldn't be printed until Monday. She even carried a drug to keep babies quiet around slave catchers. Harriet was also known to carry a pistol, not only for slave catchers but for anyone who wanted to turn back. She said, "You'll be free or you'll die." Harriet wouldn't allow anyone showing weakness to put everyone else in danger.

Harriet famously remarked, "I must've freed 1,000 slaves, but I could've freed 1,000 more if only they knew they were slaves." She returned at least 19 times to free as many people as she could, when most others wouldn't return once. Harriet became the most wanted person in America. A $40,000 reward for her arrest was issued, equivalent to more than $1.2 million today. But no one ever dared to turn Harriet in. After the Fugitive Slave Act of 1850 was passed, Harriet began taking people to Canada because more slave catchers were going into free states.

In California, the population grew rapidly after the largest unforced migration in America to date. As the Gold Rush changed the West, the California State Constitution banned slavery completely. However, states like South Carolina, Missouri, and Kentucky lifted bans on interstate slave trading. Virginia's legislature passed a law allowing slaves to be freed by will or deed, but remember, free Blacks weren't allowed in the state.

In Philadelphia, the Black population rose as more slaves escaped between 1849 and 1850. It wasn't long before white mobs started attacking them. To reinforce the institution of slavery, Missouri's legislature passed a resolution saying states should have the right to decide if slavery was legal or not. The Compromise of 1850 allowed California to enter the Union as a free state. But it allowed New Mexico and Utah to vote on legalizing slavery. The compromise banned slave trading in DC, but Maryland removed restrictions against interstate slave trading. With Maryland being the last state before slaves reached freedom, many Blacks were shipped further down south.

By 1850, the seventh U.S. Census showed America had a population of 23,191,876. Negros made up about 15 percent of the population with 3,204,313 Black enslaved people, compared to only 434,449 who were free. Many states, like Virginia, passed laws requiring free Blacks to leave within a year or face re-enslavement. In Brazil, the government declared the country would no longer participate in the slave trade. Anyone caught participating was subject to piracy charges.

Although chattel slavery was slowly being abolished globally, America strengthened its slave codes. Since so many enslaved people escaped to the North, the Fugitive Slave Act of 1850 was passed as a part of the Compromise of 1850. Doubling down on the act of 1793, the law required all runaways be returned to their owners. Despite personal liberty laws, the act of 1850 required average white citizens to be part of the slave patrol again.

Some called it the bloodhound law because of the dogs they used to track people down.

Anyone who refused to arrest an escaped person was punished, in addition to a $1,000 fine, which is about $30,000 today. Even if someone was suspected or accused of being a runaway without evidence, they were forced to arrest them or face punishment. If a Black person was accused of being a runaway, they weren't allowed to testify on their own behalf or have a jury trial.

Judges were compensated for sending people into slavery, whether they were a runaway or not. For every person they sent into slavery, they received $10. But they were only paid $5 for every person they released. If a white citizen was caught aiding a runaway by giving them food or shelter, they could face up to six months in prison, plus a $1,000 fine. Anyone who captured a Black person was given a bonus. The updated Fugitive Slave Act led to Black men, women, and children being kidnapped even more than before.

The Fugitive Slave Act also led to the price of slaves rising, especially in border states.

Many free Black people were forced to leave America and go to Canada. About 300 Black Seminoles moved to Mexico from Texas because slavery was already banned there. One of the first victims of the Fugitive Act was a free man named James Hamlet. He worked as a porter in New York, but a white guy from Maryland named Gustavus Brown accused him of running away from his mother's plantation.

James wasn't allowed to testify or speak for himself. There was no evidence James was a runaway, but he was sent to the Maryland slave market to be sold. After pamphlets telling his story were published, James was able to return home after about a week. Many people, including Frederick Douglass, used his case to condemn the Compromise of 1850. The tension was so high in America, riots exploded.

The Christiana Riot of 1851 started after Edward Gorsuch, a slave catcher, went to Pennsylvania looking for four runaways. Gorsuch considered himself a "good" slave owner, but had to hire three slave catchers to help him. He went to the home of a free Black man named William Parker looking for information. William was a runaway himself and led a Black self- defense organization to help others escape slavery. When the four men heard Gorsuch was looking for them, William offered them shelter and protection in his farmhouse.

When the slave catchers arrived at William's house, his wife sounded a horn to let them know they were there. When people heard the alarm, supporters of both sides came running with weapons. Although it isn't clear, most likely, one of Gorsuch's supporters opened fire first.

Anywhere from 50 to 100 people in William's self-defense group showed up. The four men the slave catchers were looking for refused to be taken, but Gorsuch refuse to leave without them.

Gorsuch was one of the first to be shot. His son was also shot when he ran to check on Gorsuch, but he survived. Slave owners in the area were furious and demanded the Fugitive Slave Act be enforced to set an example. Over the next few days, white mobs attacked the Black community. However, the four men were already gone, and William went to Canada with the help of Frederick Douglass. A grand jury indicted 38 people on 117 charges, including treason. This was the largest number of people charged with treason at one time in U.S. history.

William's white neighbor was also charged for helping the men escape, but he was acquitted within 15 minutes.

The Christiana Riot happened not long after Sojourner Truth gave her most famous speech, "Ain't I a Woman?" Sojourner's speech described the experience of a Black woman in America. At the same time, Harriet Beecher Stowe began publishing Uncle Tom's Cabin, although it wasn't released until 1852. Stowe was usually published in anti-slavery newspapers. Although white mobs attacked offices where anti-slave propaganda was published, Stowe's writing continued to gain popularity.

Meanwhile, slavery was officially abolished in Colombia in 1851. The next year, the Hawaiian kingdom abolished slavery. However, back in America, Texas passed a law to compensate slave owners for any enslaved person who was executed after committing a crime. Vermont passed more personal liberty laws despite the Fugitive Act, but it was only to protect white citizens. However, many vigilance committees were created to help free Negros. The Detroit Vigilance Committee helped 1,200 Black people get to Canada.

On the fourth of July 1852, Fredrick Douglass gave his famous speech, "What to the Slave is the Fourth of July?" The first live performance of Uncle Tom's Cabin also took place that year in Troy, NY. Slave states not only banned the play, but the book was banned as well. If anyone was caught selling Uncle Tom's Cabin, they were thrown in jail, if they weren't killed. The book was based on real characters and described the Black experience. It also displayed the courage of people like Josiah Henson.

Although in modern times "Uncle Tom" has become an insult, Josiah escaped from slavery with his wife and family. His right ear had been cut off after beating up a white overseer for brutally assaulting his mom. When Josiah and his family reached Canada, he started his own settlement. He even built an integrated public school, which was unheard of. Over time, Josiah helped 116 people get to freedom in Canada. With the continued success of Uncle Tom's Cabin, other books, such as Solomon Northup's book, 12 Years a Slave, were published.

Regardless of all the anti-slavery literature, an Illinois court case, Moore v. People of State of Illinois, made things tougher for slaves. The court ruling created a statute, making it illegal to harbor a runaway slave or prevent them from being captured. Although Illinois was a free state, they passed laws to forbid free Blacks from entering the state. However, the Supreme Court in Oregon ruled any Black person brought into the territory would be declared free.

Although slavery was abolished in free states, free Blacks weren't treated any better if they were allowed in the state at all. In Connecticut, a white person named Prudence Crandall was arrested for conducting a school for Black girls. One of the Black Codes made it illegal for Black children from another state to attend school in Connecticut without permission. But that didn't stop Black people from educating themselves, even if they had to move to Canada to do it. In Ontario, Mary Ann Shadd became the first Black woman to publish a newspaper.

By 1854, Venezuela and Peru abolished slavery. In America, as Harriet Tubman led more people to freedom, the Kansas-Nebraska Act was passed. The act repealed the Missouri Compromise and restricted slavery above the Mason-Dixon line. It also gave states the right to decide if they'd be a free or slave state by voting, which they called popular sovereignty.

Connecticut and Rhode Island decided to pass more personal liberty laws but to protect white citizens.

However, more people were being charged under the Fugitive Slave Act. In Wisconsin, a free man named Joshua Glover was charged with being a runaway and sent into slavery. In Boston, a man named Anthony Burns was also charged and sent into slavery. By 1855, an estimated 4,000 former slaves moved to Mexico, mostly from Texas. All Black people wanted was a chance to protect and provide for themselves and their families.

In Massachusetts, segregated schools were abolished after the court case, Roberts v. Boston. The case started after a free Black man named Benjamin Roberts sued the school system. His five-year-old daughter wasn't allowed to enroll in an all-white school because she was Black. The court ruled in the state's favor and said there was no constitutional basis for the lawsuit. Massachusetts, Maine, and Michigan passed more personal liberty laws but had no interest in protecting Black residents. Down South, Georgia and Tennessee repealed laws against interstate slave trading.

In Kansas, the first election over slavery was held in 1855. But in Ohio, John Mercer Langston, the grandfather of Langston Hughes, became the first Black person elected to serve in the government. The next year, James Buchanan was elected as the 15th president of America.

Buchanan briefly owned slaves and called the issue of slavery a matter of little practical importance in his inaugural address. For slaves however, no other issue was more important.

An enslaved mixed-race woman named Margaret Garner escaped slavery with her family. After they were caught, her husband shot back at the slave catchers. He hit one of them before he was overpowered. Instead of being sent back into slavery, Margaret tried to kill herself and her children. However, she survived, along with three of her children. After the longest fugitive slave trial on record, they were eventually sent back into slavery.

In Kansas, as tension built, a white mob destroyed the town of Lawrence. In response, an abolitionist named John Brown led what was known as Bleeding Kansas. He and six others killed five members of the mob. The fighting in Kansas continued for years.

In 1856, Congress passed a law denying Negros the right to buy property on public land that had been fixed up by the state. However, the next year, laws in New Hampshire and Vermont mandated that no Black person could be denied property based on race. Vermont also abolished laws that forbade Black people from joining the militia. In Richmond, VA, things were much different. Enslaved people were forbidden from smoking, carrying canes, or being able to self-hire.

The Slave Codes also forbade one Black people from using "provoking language" or "menacing gestures" around a white person. They also weren't allowed to go into certain parts of the city or stand on the sidewalk if it inconvenienced a white person. If a Negro walked past a white person or a white person passed them, they were forced to step off the sidewalk. They called it "street etiquette." Several states, including Kansas passed more personal liberty laws but only to protect white citizens. In 1858, Kansas officially entered the Union as a free state, despite much debate.

One of the more famous debates was the seven-part Lincoln-Douglas debates. Abraham Lincoln argued against slavery, saying the Democratic party wanted to dehumanize the Negro. Although his argument was anti-slavery, it was clear he thought the Black race wasn't equal to whites. But Lincoln felt the justification of slavery would eventually be used against poor whites. By 1859, white workers in South Carolina petitioned the legislature for laws to save them from competing with Black people for jobs. Eventually, it led to the creation of racist labor unions.

Many poor whites had a hard time finding work because they were less skilled than enslaved people. Also, slaves were much cheaper than paying a white person. Many slave states even called for the slave trade to be reinstated to meet labor demands for cotton. Poor whites resented Black people even more and blamed them for all their problems. They didn't realize they were on a plantation as well, just in a different way.

CHAPTER 15.
DECLARATION OF A CIVIL WAR: THE HOMESTEAD ACT

Slave owners in the South were desperate to keep up with the growing demand for cotton. Although the slave trade was banned in America in 1808, the last known slave ship, the Clotilda landed in Mobile, AL, in 1860. During the 1850s, so many slaves escaped to New Mexico from Texas they passed a law to limit the number of Black people in the territory.

Enslaved people couldn't travel and were prohibited from testifying in court. Even slave owners' rights to arm slaves were restricted.

In Virginia, an abolitionist named John Brown came up with a plan to arm every slave in the South. He planned to attack the biggest armory in the South at Harper's Ferry. Brown's first attempt to lead an uprising failed, but he had a second opportunity, likely because he was white, and Brown took full advantage. He led a group of 20 rebels, both Black and white, and they took over the armory. Eventually, U.S. troops, led by Robert E. Lee, stormed the arsenal and killed many of the rebels, capturing Brown. Brown was charged with murder, treason, and inciting a rebellion. He was convicted and sentenced to be hung.

Many people have heard the name John Brown, but few have heard of Shields Green. Shields went by the name "Emperor" and escaped slavery in South Carolina as a young man. When he arrived in New York, Frederick Douglass gave him a place to stay and introduced him to radical abolitionists. When Emperor met John Brown, he joined the raid on Harper's Ferry, along with five other Black men. Emperor survived the raid, but he was arrested and charged with treason. They hung him a few days after John Brown.

Frederick Douglass disagreed with John Brown's tactics and declined to take part, but he had to flee to Canada to avoid being charged with helping Brown. After Brown and his followers were executed, even more laws were passed to target the free Black population. In Georgia, any free Black person convicted of vagrancy could be sold into slavery. Essentially, it was illegal for Black people to be poor or homeless, although laws made it difficult for them to make money. Additionally, Georgia outlawed the act of slave owners granting slaves freedom through their last will and testament. Within a year, Georgia completely banned slaves from possessing firearms for any reason.

By 1860, the eighth U.S. Census showed there were over 3.9 million Black people enslaved in America. But there were only 488,000 free Blacks. Arizona passed the Expulsion Act of 1860 to banish free Blacks from the territory. However, Maine, Vermont, Rhode Island, New Hampshire, and Massachusetts granted some voting rights to free Black men and allowed them to take part in elections. With more free Blacks voting, Abraham Lincoln was elected as the first Republican president, despite the tension between the North and the South.

The South was making a fortune from cotton and tobacco, and the North wanted in on the profits. But many poor white Southerners were unable to afford owning slaves. They were already angry that slaves and free Blacks were "taking" the jobs, and the North's plan to raise taxes sent many over the edge.

To calm tensions, Abraham Lincoln wrote a letter to North Carolina Congressman John Gilmer, reassuring him he had no plans to end slavery in DC. Lincoln also said he didn't intend to stop interstate slave trading, and even if he were to recommend it, Congress wouldn't listen. He felt the Confederacy's belief that slavery was justified and should be extended opposed to the Union's belief that slavery was wrong and should be restricted wasn't enough reason for them to be angry with each other. But the South was already preparing to secede from the Union once Lincoln was elected.

In hopes of keeping the Union together, James Buchanan blamed the North for interfering with the institution of slavery in his State of the Union address. However, he said any one person being elected president isn't a just reason to dissolve the Union. Still, by the end of 1860, North Carolina voted 169 to 0 to secede from the Union. Soon, many states, including Mississippi, Florida, Alabama, Georgia, Louisiana, Texas,

Arkansas, Tennessee, and Virginia, all followed suit. In response, Congress tried to pass amendments to protect the institution of slavery, but the states didn't ratify any.

By 1861, the Civil War was officially on. Representatives from seven states that already seceded from the Union met in Alabama, where they created and ratified the Confederate Constitution. Unlike the U.S. Constitution, they directly addressed the issue of slavery. One article declared no law could be passed denying someone the right to own enslaved people.

Jefferson Davis, who was elected president of the Confederacy, said slavery was necessary to self-preservation in his inaugural speech. His vice president, Alexander Stephens, said his government rested upon the great truth that the Negro is not equal to the white man, and slavery and subordination to the superior race is a natural and normal condition.

Stephens also said their government was the first in the history of the world based upon that "great physical, philosophical, and moral truth." As for the North, a Massachusetts senator and a general in the Union Army, Benjamin Butler, declared runaway slaves to be "contraband of war." Butler refused to enforce the Fugitive Slave Act since it didn't apply to foreign countries, which the Confederacy claimed to be. Abraham Lincoln, however, made it clear and repeatedly said his war was about taxes and not about slavery at all.

Lincoln said, "I have no purpose, directly or indirectly interfering with the institution of slavery in states where it exists. I have no lawful right to do so, and I have no inclination to do so." Lincoln also said his policy was only to collect tax revenue before issuing the Morrill Tariff Act of 1861. The Morrill Tariff Act imposed a 40 percent federal sales tax on imports in slave states.

Lincoln decided to make the first move by calling for 75,000 people to enlist in the army for three months. Free Blacks in the North demanded the right to serve in the Union Army as well, but they were turned away. However, Congress eventually passed the first Confiscation Act of 1861. The Confiscation Act declared all slaves in Confederate territory occupied by the Union free, and they were no longer obligated to their enslaver. A Union general in Missouri named John Fremont confiscated Confederate property and said he'd free any slaves who took up arms against the Confederacy.

Lincoln eventually overruled Fremont. He said freeing enslaved people would alarm his Southern friends and turn them against the Union. At the time, Kentucky declared itself neutral, but Lincoln feared he'd lose them to the Confederacy. But after the Union lost battle after battle, the secretary of the Navy, Gideon Welles, accepted Black people, free or enslaved. Lincoln eventually proposed a bill to compensate slave owners who released slaves in Delaware.

However, the bill was never introduced, and slavery continued as usual in Delaware and other Northern states.

By 1860, there were over 3,000 Black slave owners on record. Most were able to buy their loved ones but were still considered owners. There were only a few Black enslavers who owned more than 65 slaves, including 6 in Louisiana. In New Orleans, a Black woman named

C. Richards owned 152 slaves. At one point, she operated a large sugar plantation with her son

P.C. Richards and became the biggest slave owner in New Orleans at the time. Some Black women even inherited slaves and other property from their enslavers.

There were five or six African Americans who were major slave owners with their own plantations. In the 1820s, John Carruthers Stanly was the richest free Negro in North Carolina. He owned three turpentine plantations and 163 slaves. John also had two white overseers, but used loyal slaves and spies to keep them in line. He was said to be a cruel owner, and his captives constantly ran away.

Like his white counterparts, he had no problem selling children or separating families.

He even held free Blacks in bondage, although the same thing could've happened to him. When anyone tried to escape, he had no problem hunting them down.

But most Black enslavers owned their loved ones. Many cases were similar to Dilsey Pope's, who was born a free woman. Dilsey bought the rights to a man she loved so they could get married. She owned her land and her home and hired out her husband to work so they could make money. But one day, Dilsey and her husband got into an argument, and she sold him to a white neighbor out of spite. When she calmed down and went to apologize and buy him back, her white neighbor refused to sell him and kept him as their property.

There was also Jacob Gasken. Jacob was born free because his mother was free; but his father was still enslaved. When Jacob got older, he and his mother saved and eventually bought his father. But one day, Jacob was being scolded and disciplined by his father after misbehaving.

Jacob became so angry he sold him. He even bragged to others that he sent his dad to work on a Louisiana plantation to "learn him some manners."

In Kentucky, a Black woman named Aunt Fanny Canady bought her own freedom. She also bought several family members, including her husband Jim who was often drunk. One day, Fanny was angry with her husband and went to his shop and told him if he didn't get it together, she was going to sell him down the river.

However, there were people like Nat Butler, a Black slave owner from Maryland. He convinced slaves to run away and hide in his home while talking to their enslavers to find out how much they'd pay to get them back. Then he'd turn in the person he convinced to escape to collect the reward. If the reward wasn't enough, he'd sell them to other slave traders at a higher price. Nat became so notorious for his actions he lost the trust of everyone, Black and white, and many tried to kill him.

Then there were slavers like William Ellison in South Carolina. By 1860, William was the wealthiest African American and one of the biggest slave owners in the state. William's mother was a slave, and his father was her enslaver. This was often the experience for enslaved Black women in a rape culture that produced many children. Although William was mulatto, he accepted and adopted the slaver mentality of his dad. Yet, he was still counted as a Black person on the Census. Unlike the French who used mixed-race children as a buffer class, in most cases in America, whites disowned and enslaved their own children. Sometimes they even sold them. In America, anyone with a drop of "Negro" blood was seen as Black.

Many biracial women and girls were sold alongside Black women and girls to be concubines. Often referred to as "fancy girls," they were seen as a status symbol for white males. The biggest markets for this were in New Orleans and Lexington, KY. Teenage girls were considered the most valuable and just as expensive as the most prime field slave. They often paid over $1,500 for them, equivalent to $30,000 today.

In Missouri, a 19-year-old enslaved biracial woman named Celia went to trial for killing her enslaver, Robert Newsom. Newsom bought Celia at the age of 14 to be a concubine. He raped her for over five years until she turned 19. He even had two children with her. When Celia turned 19, she fell in love with an enslaved man named George. After she was pregnant with her third child, Celia wasn't sure if it was George's or Newsom's baby.

Instead of stopping it himself, George threatened to break up with Celia if she kept allowing Newsom to rape her. Celia tried to ask Newsom's daughter for help, but she refused. So the next time Newsom attempted to have his way with her, she killed him in self-defense, then burned his body. Celia was arrested, but she argued it was self-defense at the trial. A Missouri law gave any woman taken against her will the right to defend herself, and even murder was justifiable. But the judge, William Hall, ruled against her. He said since she was slave property, the law to protect women didn't apply to her. Celia was eventually found guilty and executed by hanging in 1855.

A few years before Celia's case, another enslaved biracial woman, also named Celia, was the first woman executed on record in Florida in 1848. She was enslaved by her own father, Jacob Bryan. Bryan constantly abused and raped Celia, like any other enslaved woman. Bryan was likely the father of her children and possibly her younger sister Ann's children as well.

When Celia was 30, she killed Bryan by splitting his head open with a drawknife. She tried to flee, but she was arrested the next day.

During her trial, she argued self-defense because Bryan tried to discipline her while she was working in the field. Although a jury convicted her of manslaughter, they recommended executive clemency. However, the judge, Thomas Douglas, ignored the jury's recommendation and sentenced her to be hung. Citing a Florida statute from an 1840 Act,

Douglas said if any slave or free Negro or mulatto, shall be guilty of manslaughter of any white person, they shall suffer death. Although Celia's execution was postponed, she was still lynched on September 22, 1848.

In most cases, the biracial children of slave owners were made into field slaves or sold off. In other cases, they were made into house slaves and given more benefits than others, including being exempt from the same physical labor as field slaves. On even rarer occasions, they were accepted and claimed by their father, like in the case of William Ellison.

Originally known as April Ellison, William became an apprentice to a cotton gin maker at the age of ten. He also learned other skills, such as blacksmithing, and made enough money to buy his freedom. Most of his earnings went to his enslaver, but it became common practice for some in South Carolina and Louisiana to pay enslaved people for any work done on Sundays.

After buying his freedom at the age of 26, he changed his name from April to William, after his father and enslaver. He eventually started his own cotton gin business and owned 63 slaves, making him the largest mixed-race slaver in South Carolina.

As the Civil War broke out, William pledged allegiance to the Confederacy. He offered his slaves for their use and grew crops on his plantation to supply food instead of cotton.

William's son even tried to join the Confederate Army but was denied because he was still seen as a Negro. Despite being a former slave and viewed as Black, William was said to be as harsh as any white slaver. While colorism still affects us worldwide today, at times, biracial people have a hard time identifying or being accepted by one side or the other. In William's case, he identified more with his father and enslaver. But today, William is used as an example of one of the few successful Black slave owners.

In 1861, Harriet Ann Jacobs published her autobiography Incidents in the Life of a Slave Girl. Harriet was born to two enslaved biracial parents in 1813. She was the first enslaved woman to write an autobiographical narrative on slavery, joining the likes of Frederick Douglass. Her story was one of the earliest to highlight the treatment and sexual abuse of

Black and biracial women. She said even a little child blessed with beauty quickly learned that, for a Black girl, it was a curse. Not only were they targeted more by white males, they also had to deal with jealousy from white women because they were often favored by their husbands. And judges repeatedly made it clear there was no such thing as rape when it came to Black women.

Harriet's enslaver, James Norcom, began sexually abusing her from around the age of

12. He'd already fathered 11 enslaved children and sold most of them. In some cases, like with Harriet, Black women tried to get white males to marry or fall in love with them, hoping it would lead to freedom. Harriet's husband tried to buy her freedom, along with her children. Norcom not only refused, but he became angry. He threatened to send her children to a brutal plantation where slaves were usually sent to be broken. To save them, Harriet was forced to leave them behind. She hid in a tiny crawl space in the attic of her grandmother's house for years before she managed to escape to freedom in New York.

Meanwhile, as Texas seceded from the Union in 1861, they outlawed granting slaves freedom completely, even in a last will and testament. Florida reinforced laws to give average white citizens on slave patrol more authority to search the homes of free and enslaved Blacks at any time and to confiscate any weapons found. Yet, as Southern states continued to secede, Congress admitted Kansas into the Union as the 34th state and a free territory.

West Virginia was admitted the next year as a free state. But since the territory was considered a part of Virginia before, there were still people enslaved. But West Virginia's state Constitution called for gradual emancipation. As Utah also abolished slavery in 1862, Congress followed suit by abolishing slavery in Washington, DC. The bill that was signed by Abraham Lincoln freed more than 3,000. However, the bill gave slave owners reparations by compensating them with an average of $300 for every enslaved person they lost.

Lincoln approved another bill to prohibit Union soldiers from returning runaway or captured slaves to anyone unless they were loyal to the Union. He asked the four Northern border states to offer compensated emancipation, but they refused and rejected his plan. But America signed the Lyons-Seward Treaty of 1862 with Britain to suppress the slave trade aggressively. Although there was much undocumented, illegal slave trading, only one U.S. citizen named Nathaniel Gordon was found guilty and put to death.

Lastly, Lincoln approved a bill to appoint representatives to establish relations with Haiti and Liberia. Those were the only Black nations recognized by the U.S. Lincoln's goal was to hurt the South, but he was clear it was about the war, not justice or freedom for Black people.

Lincoln said in a letter, "If I could save the Union without freeing any slaves, I would do it; and if I could save it by freeing all the slaves I would do it; and if I could save it by freeing some and leaving others alone, I would also do that."

One Union general in South Carolina issued General Order No. 11 to free any captive in South Carolina, Georgia, and Florida if they helped the Union fight. It would've freed over 900,000, people but Lincoln overruled and nullified the order. He said no general or any person not authorized by the U.S. Government could declare any slave in any state to be free. Congress offered compensated emancipation to slave owners in states loyal to the Union, if they chose.

Lincoln signed into law a resolution to prohibit slavery on all federal territories. But for white citizens, he passed an act that drastically changed the landscape of America. The Homestead Act of 1862 essentially gave 270 million acres or 10 percent of the land in the U.S. away to citizens who remained loyal to the Union. Originally, the Homestead Act wasn't limited to just white males, it was also available for single women and free Blacks. But to make a claim for 160 acres of free land, people had to pledge not to take up arms against the Union.

The only other requirements to receive land were you had to be 21, the head of a household, and live on and upkeep the land for at least five years. Once you'd met the requirements and paid a total of $18, the land was yours. There was a $10 filing fee, a $2 commission, and after five years, another $6 fee, before receiving a deed for the land signed by the president. Although, technically, the Homestead Act was originally supposed to be for everyone, Lincoln and many others still didn't recognize Black people as actual citizens or equals.

He didn't want to appear desperate for help from Negros. He turned down three Black regiments from Massachusetts and Rhode Island, despite all his efforts to recruit soldiers. But Lincoln was at a disadvantage because the Confederacy had far more resources. The South began winning more battles than Lincoln expected, like the Battle of Fredericksburg. Out of 70,000 soldiers, the Union lost over 12,600. After the Battle of Antietam, one of the bloodiest battles in American history, the Union started losing hope and Lincoln had to rethink his strategy.

Although he didn't see Black people as equals, and he feared arming and training Black soldiers, he had no choice. Like with previous wars, accepting and arming Black soldiers was a last resort. But pride comes before the fall. So like his predecessor George Washington, he was forced to beg them to help him fight in exchange for freedom.

CHAPTER 16.
AN EMANCIPATION PROCLAMATION: THE DRAFT RIOTS

With Abraham Lincoln taking over as president, it was now his turn to deal with the "Negro question" in America. Lincoln made it clear he felt Blacks shouldn't have social or political equity with whites. He believed colonization was the best answer. He said with the differences between the races and the hostility of whites toward Blacks, it would be better to separate.

In 1862, Lincoln hosted a delegation of free Blacks. It was the first time an American president met with representatives of the Black community in public to discuss racial issues. Lincoln's goal was to try to convince them to leave the U.S. and go to Central America or Liberia. But the Black delegation was angry. They argued Black people were just as native to this country as whites and were entitled and deserved to enjoy the same rights.

Although Lincoln didn't agree, the Union continued losing battles to the Confederacy. Eventually, he passed the Militia Act of 1862. The Militia Act finally allowed Blacks to join or work for the U.S. Army. It also offered freedom to any enslaved person in Confederate territory if they were able to escape and help the union fight. Many Black leaders, including Harriet Tubman and Moses Dickson, organized Black troops and recruited more soldiers for the Union. Although the Confederacy forced Black women to work in hospitals, thousands voluntarily joined the Union as spies, nurses, and laundresses. Many others made it difficult for slave owners by running away or refusing to work.

With a newfound hope of freedom, even more captives escaped North to take up arms and fight. There were many Black heroes in the Civil War, although most went unrecognized. An enslaved man named Robert Smalls took over a Confederate ship and helped deliver it to the

Union Army. Understanding he had no choice, Lincoln called for 300,000 volunteers, both Black and white, to join the militia for nine months.

Not long after that, and for the first time publicly, Lincoln announced his preliminary plan for his Emancipation Proclamation. Essentially, the Proclamation was an executive order that declared all persons held as slaves in states rebelling against the Union shall be free from now on and forever. Of course, his Proclamation didn't apply to states that were loyal to the Union. It didn't even apply to Confederate areas under Union control, with Lincoln hoping whites in those states would become loyal. Since it only applied to Confederate states that seceded and were no longer part of America, his Proclamation didn't free anyone.

In response, Jefferson Davis signed an executive order of his own. His orders were to treat any Black soldiers captured as rebelling slaves and not as prisoners of war. The Confederate Congress also amended the draft exemption law. Slave owners and overseers on plantations with over 20 enslaved people were exempt from being drafted into the Confederate Army. Many slavers in the South moved to Texas with their captives to avoid the Union Army and their offer for freedom. The U.S. Attorney General issued a ruling that declared freedmen born in the U.S. were considered citizens. But Lincoln was still against arming Blacks or letting them fight in the war.

Even though Black people weren't physically able to fight in the war, they used the opportunity to demand land of their own. The Freedman's Association demanded Lincoln give free Blacks the seized land in the Sea Islands in South Carolina. They accessed tiny amounts of land to start working for themselves as a rehearsal for reconstruction. In Mississippi, there was also the Davis Bend experiment where free Blacks controlled their own community.

After the Union seized Jefferson Davis's brother's plantation, Ulysses S. Grant told his officers to make it a Negro plantation. Former slaves worked together to farm the land and build their own community. They also made nice profits by selling cotton and other produce. While free Blacks attempted to build something of their own in Mississippi, one of the first civil rights leaders, Ida B. Wells, was born enslaved there in 1862. Meanwhile, in Ohio, Mary Jane Patterson became the first Black woman to graduate college in America after graduating from Oberlin College.

On January 1, 1863, Lincoln officially signed the Emancipation Proclamation. Since it only applied to Confederate states, he had no power to enforce it, and it freed no one. In fact, he said it wouldn't apply to any state that rejoined the Union, hoping to get them on his side.

Southern newspapers like the Richmond Enquirer wrote, "This is the most startling political crime and stupidest political blunder yet known in American history," and "Southern people now can only choose between victory and death."

Attempting to calm the outrage, Lincoln said the states that were not included still have the rights and privileges they've always had, including slavery. Losses continued for Lincoln and the Union Army. Yet, he refused to arm Black soldiers. Eventually, he was forced to create the first federal draft. Around 162,535 males between the ages of 20 and 40 were drafted. Congress also passed a bill to allow 150,000 Colored soldiers to enlist.

In 1863, the American Freedman's Inquiry Commission was created to interview freed slaves in the South about the conditions they lived in. In a report from 1864, their findings included the racism Black soldiers faced in the Union Army. Despite Lincoln's Proclamation, some Union soldiers illegally held runaway slaves until their enslaver came for them, even though they had agreed to fight against the Confederacy. Sometimes, the soldiers forced the enslaver to pay money to get them back, or they sold them to someone else for a larger profit. The report also described the poverty and brutal conditions former enslaved people faced in the

U.S. There were many cases of Union soldiers stealing from poverty-stricken Black soldiers. Frederick Douglass requested a private meeting with Lincoln for the first time to discuss the treatment of Black soldiers and Black people in America. Lincoln realized he had no choice but to arm Black soldiers to win the war, despite his fear of armed Negros. The first all-Black regiment, the 54th Massachusetts Infantry, was made up of the first armed Black soldiers who joined the war. The movie Glory was based on their story. As Robert E. Lee's troops continued to march north, it caused panic in Union territories. Lincoln had no choice but to turn to Black soldiers for help.

Both of Frederick Douglass's sons joined the infantry. Harriet Tubman helped Union troops free over 700 slaves in South Carolina herself. Many took up arms and helped the Union fight. Despite changing the tide of the war, many white citizens were angry the Union armed and allowed Black soldiers to fight. Poor whites, mostly immigrants, were so upset it led to violent race wars in multiple cities, lasting over a week.

In Detroit, white immigrants, including many Irish immigrants, were already agitated about being drafted to fight in the war. They felt they were being forced to fight for the benefit of Black people in the South. After Lincoln's Proclamation, the Detroit Free Press published multiple articles blaming Negros for labor problems, citizenship issues, and the war itself.

Newspapers constantly ran stories linking Blacks to crime and to having no morals overall. They especially ran stories telling whites to beware of the big bad Black man raping the helpless white woman.

Many of these immigrants feared competing for jobs with Black people. They saw Black people as a threat to the working-class white male. On March 6, 1863, after white mobs attacked Black residents, one paper reported it as the bloodiest day in Detroit. It started after a newspaper published a story about a Negro raping a young white girl. A biracial man named William Faulkner was accused of raping a nine-year-old girl named Mary Brown.

Although William referred to himself as Spanish and Indian and didn't identify as Black, once he was accused, the paper immediately labeled him a Negro. As far as whites were concerned, he was nothing but a "nigger" who'd raped a white girl, whether it was true or not.

Amid his trial, a lynch mob gathered at the courthouse. During the second day, they attacked random Black people in the area.

Without any evidence besides the word of a nine-year-old girl, William was convicted and sentenced to life in prison. As he was transported to prison, the mob tried to take him so they could lynch him. The guard fired into the crowd in an attempt to stop them, but he killed someone in the mob. The group became even more furious that a white German was killed at the trial for a Black man. They attacked random Black people in their communities, targeting men, women, and children, and they destroyed businesses and homes.

One man named Joshua Boyd was hit in the head with an ax as he tried to escape a building they'd set on fire. The crowd looted businesses and homes and stole anything they thought was valuable. They also robbed any Black person they saw in the streets. By the end, countless people were killed and many more injured. Over 200 homes and businesses were destroyed. Most Black residents left for Canada. William Faulkner survived the riot but went to prison. Years later, Mary Brown recanted her story and admitted she'd lied. Although she was never punished, William was released from prison and went on to start his own produce business in Detroit.

As a result of the riot, Detroit established its own full-time police force, which remained all-white until relatively recent times. Detroit wasn't the only place experiencing violent race riots as a result of Lincoln's draft. In New York, the Draft Riots of 1863 broke out around the same time. White immigrants, especially the Irish, were angry about being drafted and planned to take it out on the Black communities.

The mayor, Fernando Wood, was so angry he suggested New York secede from the Union as well. White residents already refused to work alongside Black people, but by March, it escalated to physical attacks. When the official draft was held in July, over 1,200 people, mostly Irish immigrants, were drafted. As they gathered in bars to drink and complain about the draft, they decided to protest it. It wasn't long before they burned down the building the draft office was in, and soon, they'd destroyed other buildings.

Since most of the troops were off to war, there were only about 800 guards left to stop them. But their numbers grew quickly to around 50,000. They targeted abolitionists or anyone classified as a "nigger lover." In the beginning, the damage was limited to destroying and burning down businesses. But then they turned their attention toward Black people. White men, women, and children looted an orphanage for Black children before burning it down. They pillaged and destroyed many homes and businesses, including James McCune Smith's pharmacy, possibly the first Black-owned pharmacy in America.

The rowdy group walked the street, looking for any Black person they could find. They beat and lynched a Black man before setting him on fire as he was coming from a bakery with only a loaf of bread in his hands. The mob blamed Black people for all of their problems, and their goal was to drive them out, even if they had to commit genocide to do it. One hundred twenty people were reported killed, but some estimate that thousands of people may have been murdered during the riot. Thousands more left the city, and the Black population fell to under 11,000 for the first time since 1820.

The Draft Riots continued to spread from Boston to Ohio, although not as violent as the riot in New York. The rioting in Ohio was already occurring in 1862. It started after two Black men got into a heated argument with a group of white guys. They accused one of the Black men of striking a white man in the head with a block of wood. The group quickly turned into a mob, and they attacked every Black person in the area.

Some Black men fought back and wounded some members of the group. As time passed, whites citizens continued to attack Black people randomly, ambushing them as they walked down the street. Their goal was to intimidate Black residents into leaving the state so they wouldn't have to compete with them. They complained that Negros were interfering with their labor strikes. But unlike the German immigrants who were scared away, Black people were still willing to work, so they felt a need to resort to violence.

The anger from Northern and Southern states grew as the war dragged on. After two years, the number of casualties was adding up. Between the Emancipation Proclamation, the draft, and the arming of Black soldiers, things were reaching a boiling point. But this bloody war seemed to have no end in sight until the Battle of Gettysburg. The battle lasted three days, and it was one of the bloodiest battles in American history. Over 10,000 people died, and more than 40,000 were wounded.

As soon as Lincoln began accepting Black troops, the tide of the war immediately turned. Robert E. Lee's troops were pushed back, and he realized how much Black troops strengthened the Union Army. In response, the Confederate Government threatened to capture Black soldiers and put them back into slavery or execute them. Since many Black soldiers escaped to help the Union fight, Lincoln declared the government would give the same protection to any soldier, no matter the race. For every Black soldier sold into slavery, a rebel soldier was to be put into hard labor. For every Black soldier killed, a rebel soldier was to be put to death.

Lincoln even wrote a letter to Ulysses S. Grant saying, "[Colored troops are] a resource which, if vigorously applied now, will soon close the contest." But he wasn't the only one who recognized the difference Black troops were making. The Alabama State Legislature authorized using enslaved Blacks in the Confederate Army, although the last thing they wanted to do was arm them. When Confederate soldiers attacked Lawrence, KS, they killed 150 civilians and caused over $500,000 in damage. Lincoln met with people like Frederick Douglass and the governor of Maryland to discuss recruiting more Black soldiers.

With Lincoln still calling for 300,000 people to enlist, he was invited to give a speech in Gettysburg, otherwise known as "The Gettysburg Address." The Federal War Department also established the Bureau of Colored Troops for Black soldiers. Hoping to end the war, Lincoln issued a Proclamation of Amnesty and Reconstruction. He offered a pardon to anyone who participated in this treasonous rebellion if they became loyal to the Union. Although it didn't end the war, he also issued another proclamation declaring the last Thursday in November to be a day of Thanksgiving.

Meanwhile, overseas, Lincoln made a treaty with Liberia to establish trading. In the Netherlands, the Dutch finally abolished slavery in all its colonies in 1863. In Africa, the French tried to expand to the west in areas near Senegal. In 1859, France attacked the Tukulor Empire until they were forced to give up much of their land and relocate to modern-day Mali. Al-Hajj Umar, who established the empire, fought back against the French, and even took control of Timbuktu. However, he was killed in 1863 after his army was defeated by the Tuaregs, the Moors, and the Fulani.

Back in America, by 1864, 400,000 enslaved people escaped after making it behind Union Army lines, and many signed up to join the fight. Lincoln proposed a plan for slave owners to free their captives in exchange for fighting. He even asked them to hire their former slaves for fair pay and treat them the same as white workers. But Lincoln still called for another 500,000 people to enlist, including Black people. He asked for volunteers to serve in the Army for three years, or until the war ended. Congress even approved an act to compensate slave owners in border states who remained loyal to the Union if their slaves were drafted.

But a senator from Missouri named John B. Henderson was the first to propose the 13th Amendment to abolish slavery. After Lincoln was nominated for his second term as president, he called for another draft to recruit 200,000 more soldiers into his army. Following a meeting with Ulysses S. Grant, Lincoln gave him full control of the Union Army.

When Louisiana's State Constitution abolished slavery in 1864, Lincoln wrote a letter congratulating the governor on being the first to govern Louisiana as a free state. As the Union gained control of the war, Arkansas and Tennessee also adopted new constitutions to abolish slavery under Lincoln's 10 percent plan for reconstruction. This plan offered forgiveness to Confederate states and allowed them to be readmitted into the Union after at least 10 percent of voters pledged allegiance to the Union. Voters were also allowed to elect delegates to establish new state constitutions and governments. All Southerners involved in the rebellion, except high- ranking Confederate officials and soldiers, were granted a full pardon. All their property, except slaves, were returned.

The U.S. Senate passed the 13th Amendment with a vote of 38 to 6. The 13th amendment said, "Neither slavery nor involuntary servitude, except as punishment for crime whereof the party shall have been duly convicted, shall exist within the United States, or any place subject to their jurisdiction." Of course, this didn't actually end slavery, as movies like 13th demonstrate. However, few mention the part about involuntary servitude and what that really means. As Black people would soon find out, they were still dealing with slavery, just under a different name.

A few days after the 13th Amendment was passed, a Confederate general called for the massacre of "colored" troops in Tennessee. They slaughtered 262 Black soldiers, although most of them tried to surrender. Black soldiers didn't get the same protection or pay they were entitled to. Lincoln passed the Equalization Bill to ensure they received the same pay as white soldiers. They were entitled to partial back pay, but it didn't go into effect until 1865.

Congress also voted on a resolution to abolish slavery completely, but it failed, with a vote of 95 to 66. When Lincoln formally accepted the nomination for president at the Maryland Constitutional Convention, slavery in the territory was finally abolished with a vote of 30,174 to 29,799, a difference of 375 votes. Lincoln eventually signed an act to repeal the Fugitive Slave Acts of 1793 and 1850, along with other laws referring to runaway slaves.

After Congress passed the Wade-Davis Reconstruction Bill, 50 percent of the white male population was required to take a loyalty oath before they were readmitted to the Union. The bill also outlawed slavery and gave Black people the right to vote. However, high-ranking Confederate officials still weren't allowed to vote. Lincoln opposed the bill because he feared Confederate rebels wouldn't accept it. The Wade-Davis Bill also gave Congress control over reconstruction instead of the president.

The fighting continued, and Lincoln was still calling for 500,000 soldiers to volunteer. In response, Jefferson Davis recommended the Confederate Government buy slaves to fight with them. Davis also promised to free them at the end of the war. Lincoln continued to meet with Frederick Douglass to recruit more Black soldiers. He also met with Sojourner Truth to discuss ways to announce the 13th Amendment. Not only did Lincoln want to end the war, he also wanted the Black vote to ensure he'd get reelected

Eventually, Lincoln was reelected president. Congress also admitted Nevada into the Union as the 36th state in 1864. Nebraska had the chance to be adopted into the Union that year but failed to create a state constitution that complied with certain conditions.

As the North took control of the war, General William Sherman's army marched through the South to capture and destroy Confederate territories. Over 17,000 slaves were freed by Sherman's army in South Carolina, Georgia, and Florida. About 8,000 former enslaved people helped him take the city of Savannah, GA, and freed nearly 7,000 more. General Sherman sent a telegraph to Lincoln saying the city of Savannah was a Christmas gift to him.

After Louisiana abolished slavery, The New Orleans Tribune was established. It was one of the first Black newspapers to publish daily. In Boston, Rebecca Ann Crumple became the first Black woman to earn a medical degree and the first Black woman to become a doctor in America.

As the Dominican Republic declared independence from Spain in 1865, the Union was on the brink of winning the war. The Confederacy debated if they should start arming Black people as well. The Confederate Congress became increasingly unhappy with Jefferson Davis and his administration. Once the Union armed Black soldiers, the Confederacy's hopes of winning the war quickly faded.

CHAPTER 17.
JUNETEENTH: 40 ACRES AND A MULE

Although the U.S. Senate passed the 13th Amendment in 1864, it failed in the House of Representatives with a vote of 93 to 65. However, by 1865, Tennessee and Missouri adopted Amendments to abolish slavery in their state constitutions. As the North gained control of the war, General William Sherman issued Special Field Order No. 15. The order called for 400,000 acres of land in South Carolina, Georgia, and Florida to be confiscated and redistributed to the freedmen who fought in the war.

Special Field Order No. 15, later known as the promise for 40 acres and a mule, was supposed to give newly freed enslaved people sole and exclusive management of their communities. No white person, except soldiers on duty, was allowed to live on the land. The order was issued after Sherman met with local leaders in the Black community who were still angry about the Ebenezer Creek Massacre.

Sherman's army marched through Georgia in what was known as Sherman's March to the Sea. As the Confederacy continued to be pushed back, many slavers abandoned their plantations, and thousands of slaves were freed. The Union Army used the newly freed slaves, who were able to work to clear the land and make it passable for the troops and their equipment. They were often referred to as the pioneers. Those who were unable to work, mostly the women, children, and elderly, followed the troops for protection. They were referred to as contraband.

The Union soldiers felt the contraband slowed them down and created too many problems. With Confederate troops led by Joseph Wheeler quickly approaching, Union troops led by Jefferson C. Davis reached Ebenezer Creek and were unable to cross. Davis ordered his troops to help the pioneers build a bridge as quickly as possible, and by midnight it was finished. Davis posted guards on the bridge and told the contraband to wait until all the troops and equipment were over the bridge before they came across. Once the troops and the pioneers were clear, Davis gave the order to dismantle the bridge. He told the guards not to let a single Negro cross.

Davis left helpless women, children, and elderly in a death trap. Many panicked as Confederate troops closed in. Wheeler and his troops showed no mercy and slaughtered them. Several hundred, if not thousands, of people chose to jump in the icy water rather than face Confederate troops, even though many couldn't swim. Countless people drowned trying to make it across as Confederate soldiers fired their guns at them.

Those who didn't jump in the water may have suffered an even worse fate. Chaos ensued as soon as Confederate troops arrived. Many were crushed in the initial stampede. The soldiers shot, slashed, and tortured women, children, and the elderly. One witness said, "Cries of anguish and despair, men, women, children rushed by the hundreds into the turbid stream, and many were drowned before our eyes. From what we learned afterward of those who remained on land, their fate at the hands of Wheeler's troops was scarcely to be preferred."

Thousands of people were slaughtered, and some were returned to slavery. But Davis ordered his troops to keep marching. Some witnesses were infuriated with Davis's barbaric orders, which sparked a public outcry. In response, General Sherman and the Secretary of War, Edwin Stanton, agreed to meet with 20 freedmen who represented the Black community.

Sherman and Stanton asked them about emancipation and what it meant to them, about the war, and what they wanted for the Black community.

The group elected Garrison Frazier to be the spokesman. Sherman and Stanton guaranteed the freedmen protection and provisions until things were settled. Garrison said, "The best way we can take care of ourselves is to have land of our own … We want to be placed on land until we are able to buy it and make it our own." When asked if they'd rather live scattered among whites or in colonies of their own, Garrison replied, "I would prefer to live by ourselves, for there is prejudice against us in the South that will take years to get over."

Four days after the meeting, Special Field Order No. 15 was issued.

Within six months, 40,000 freedmen lived on 400,000 acres of coastal land. They worked for themselves, made the land productive, and quickly built their own communities. They established their own civil and educational institutions and even created a militia to protect them. To make it official, the Bureau of Refugees, Freedmen, and Abandoned Lands, later known as the Freedman's Bureau was established by an act of Congress. The Freedman's Bureau was supposed to help newly freed slaves adjust by providing food, shelter, clothing, and medical care. The Bureau was only set to last until the war ended and a year thereafter.

Lincoln eventually signed a bill to free the wives and children of Black Union soldiers. In an attempt to stop the war, he proposed a resolution to pay reparations to slave owners in 16 states. The resolution offered over $100 million as compensation, but slave owners unanimously disapproved of it.

On January 31, 1865, the 13th Amendment was officially passed. Illinois became the first state to ratify it. Maryland, New York, West Virginia, Maine, and Kansas all followed suit, although Delaware refused. Even though the 13th Amendment was official, the war still wasn't over. However, General Sherman's army took Columbia, S.C., and forced Confederate soldiers to flee. The Union Army also took control of Wilmington, NC.

After the Confederacy suffered another major defeat in Waynesboro, VA, the Confederate Senate authorized using Black soldiers by a vote of nine to eight. Although they were never officially enlisted, Jefferson Davis agreed and asked plantation owners to send captives to fight on their behalf. Still, Davis wrote a letter to Robert E. Lee saying his work with Negro troops hadn't made any progress and distrust was increasing, and it was embarrassing in many ways.

As Wisconsin and Minnesota ratified the 13th Amendment, New Jersey and Kentucky still refused. The Union made its final campaign against the Confederacy in Petersburg and Richmond, VA. Davis was forced to abandon the Confederate capital in Richmond, VA. Rebel troops lost all hope and destroyed their own capital, worse than anything the Union Army did. They burned the city to the ground.

After the Union took control of Richmond, Lincoln went on a tour of the city. Crowds of newly freed slaves praised him and called him "The Great Messiah" and "Father Abraham." Although Lincoln saw them as inferior, one man kneeled at his feet and blessed him. Another woman kissed his hand and said, "I know I am free, for I have seen Father Abraham and felt him."

After Lincoln was reelected, Black people, including Frederick Douglass, were able to attend the presidential inauguration for the first time. In his last speech, Lincoln supported limited voting rights for Black people in Southern states. But as General Sherman accepted the surrender of Confederate troops, Lincoln was shot and killed at the Ford Theater in Washington, DC by John Wilkes Booth.

Nearly 2,000 Negros demanded to be a part of Lincoln's funeral procession in New York. Not long after he was buried, Arkansas, Missouri, and Connecticut finally ratified the 13th Amendment. But after Andrew Johnson was sworn in as president, things quickly changed for the worse. Johnson immediately reversed Special Field Order No.15. He ordered the land be returned to the former slave owners and offered amnesty and pardons to many Confederate soldiers for their treason. Johnson restored all their rights, except their right to own slaves.

It wasn't until June 19, 1865, that word of the Emancipation Proclamation reached Galveston, TX. Nearly 200,000 slaves, some of whom were taken during the war, found out they were free from chattel slavery. Soon, South Carolina, Alabama, Georgia, North Carolina, and Oregon, all ratified the 13th Amendment. Yet, Mississippi still refused to do so. Instead, Mississippi passed some of the first Black Codes and established a racial hierarchy to keep Negros in their place. They didn't waste time criminalizing Black people. They feared Black people would spread out and make the white race disappear now that they were free.

Mississippi passed vagrancy and peonage laws to criminalize Black people for being poor. Negros and mulattos were required to show proof of employment or be arrested. A tax was levied only on the Black population, and if they didn't pay, they were arrested. They also had to pay the cop that arrested them five dollars. Black people were allowed to rent property only in the city to prevent them from farming independently.

It was also a crime for Black couples to live together without being married. The state gave itself the power to take Black children if they deemed the parents couldn't afford them. If the parents were arrested for vagrancy, their children were forced into apprenticeships, another form of slavery—most times with their former enslaver. Whites were even allowed to use capital punishment to discipline their "apprentices" as they saw fit. They were given the power to recapture anyone who tried to escape, similar to the Fugitive Slave Law.

It was still illegal for groups of Black people to assemble at any time. It was even illegal for whites to associate with Negros or mulattos and treat them as equals. Other laws forbade Black people from buying liquor or owning weapons. Anyone who broke the law was arrested and leased out to work for no pay. As soon as America passed the 13th Amendment, the Black Codes allowed slavery to continue through convict leasing.

In Jackson, MS, and other places like Norfolk, VA, Black people held meetings to figure out how to move forward and demand equal rights. Finally, in December 1865, the 13th Amendment was officially adopted into the Constitution. Although sharecropping would soon replace it, there are no words that could truly describe the horrors of chattel slavery and what they'd experienced. Books written by former enslaved people, as well as the slave narratives, give some insight into their experiences. Also, movies such as Mandingo and Drum depict life as a slave to some degree.

By 1860, the U.S. Census showed there were close to 4 million people enslaved in America. They were estimated to be worth more than $3.5 billion, equivalent to $106 billion today. Slaves were by far the largest and most important asset in the U.S. economy. They were worth more than all manufacturing, railroads, and every other American asset combined.

After the 13th Amendment became ratified, Oliver Howard was put in charge of the Freedman's Bureau. The organization was created to help Black people with education, health care, and in the court system. Many thought slavery was over, but it simply took a new form.

The keyword in the 13th Amendment is "except," meaning there are conditions where slavery is still legal in America. Supposedly, the North won the war, but rarely in history has the losing side been able to fly their flag on federal buildings, honor their heroes, or control their own narrative. For decades after the war, statues of Confederate leaders were erected. To this day, there are still heated debates about if they should be taken down or not. Many former Confederate soldiers and slave owners came up with an expression, "The South shall rise again." But the question is, how far did they actually fall?

Another part of the 13th Amendment that isn't often talked about is the phrase "involuntary servitude." Just by adding that phrase, it makes voluntary servitude legal. Although it affects everyone the same, by controlling the economic infrastructure in every way, you control what people are willing to work for and at what price. Add in a miseducation system and you have a recipe for things like the school to prison pipeline.

Under Andrew Johnson's reconstruction plan, only whites could vote or hold public office. However, Congress refused to acknowledge any state governments formed under the plan. Still, Mississippi passed laws to forbid Blacks from owning or carrying guns, ammunition, or Bowie knives unless they were in the military. Louisiana also passed laws to forbid Black people from owning guns unless they had permission from the police.

Before the 13th Amendment was enforced, the first Black Codes were already in full effect. Radical Republicans like Charles Sumner and Thaddeus Stevens, who had a Black mistress and mixed-race children, argued that former slaves needed more help from the government. They said, "You can't release all of these slaves with no money, no food, no land, no animals, no weapons, or anything and then say they are free." They also said, "If you turn loose all these Negros without giving them something, they will always be slaves." They suggested giving Black people 40 acres and a mule along with $100 as a form of reparations.

However, when Sumner and Stevens proposed legislation, Andrew Johnson quickly vetoed it. Johnson said, "Negros are free and don't need any handouts; let the niggers work or starve." Many white Southerners feared losing free labor, and feared competing for jobs even more. South Carolina soon followed Mississippi's lead and forbid Black people from owning guns or weapons. South Carolina also required Negros to pay a bond for "good behavior" before they were allowed in the state. It was illegal for Black people to make or sell liquor or any farm products. They weren't even allowed to sell what they grew without permission from a white employer. They claimed it was to keep them from stealing.

In South Carolina, it was illegal for Black people to have any occupation except as a farmer in a sharecropping contract unless they received a license from a judge. Licenses to work had to be renewed every year, and most likely, they had to pay money to get it. Then, after heavily restricting Black people's ability to earn money, the state harshly enforced vagrancy and peonage laws to incarcerate and re-enslave them.

The law allowed the sheriff to arrest homeless Black people and hire out them out as he saw fit. The law also forced the children of anyone arrested into apprenticeships against their will. Often, they were forced to work for their former enslaver until the age of 21 for males and 18 for females. The law also gave white males the right to punish Black children for their behavior. If they tried to escape, white males could punish them however they chose. Plantation owners were obligated by law to feed, clothe, and send Black children to school. They were also required to teach them a trade.

Not only was being homeless or unemployed against the law, loitering, gambling, and peddling, or being a traveling salesman, was also illegal. Black people weren't allowed to be on juries or to testify in court against a white person. Crimes like arson, rebellion, and burglary, even something as minor as stealing a pig out of hunger, resulted in the death penalty. Of course, being accused of assaulting a white person or looking at a white woman was punishable by death, even without evidence.

Black people had a few more rights they didn't have during slavery, but they were heavily restricted. They could acquire land, own property, enter contracts, sue or be sued, and earn money. Marriage between Black men and women was also now recognized by the government. However, interracial marriage was still outlawed, especially between a Black man and a white woman.

Of course, the right to vote was limited to white males only. But the Black Codes applied to every "person of color." South Carolina defined "persons of color" as anyone with more than one-eighth Negro blood. If you had more than one Black great-grandparent, you were considered a "person of color" and the Black Codes applied. Congress initially rejected the Black Codes and accused white Southerners of trying to re-institute slavery.

The Freedman's Bureau argued that the Black Codes were invalid. Under the guise of reconstruction, the Bureau went to the South to provide food, welfare, and to help Black Southerners adjust to life after slavery. In reality, the Freedman's Bureau was used to set up sharecropping contracts between Black Southerners and their former enslavers. Many Black people were unable to read or write and were tricked into signing away their freedom with these contracts.

The American economy still depended on cotton and tobacco produced by slave labor.

So the Freedman's Bureau, along with the government, threatened to withhold food and other resources meant to help Black people unless they signed the contract. Once signed, Black workers weren't allowed to quit, protest, strike for better conditions, or demand higher wages. Plantation owners were obligated to provide the land, seeds, and animals. At the end of the year, workers were paid based on how much they produced. However, Black farmers were allowed to sell only what they produced to the white plantation owner.

Although white planters could sell the produce to anyone and make as much profit as possible, Black farmers were only paid what white plantation owners decided to pay them.

White planters also kept the books so Black farmers didn't know how much money they were shorted. By the end of the year, Black farmers rarely made a profit. In fact, in most cases, they were in debt to the plantation owners. To pay it off, they had to work for free until they produced enough to cover their debt. Of course, they were never able to produce enough to get out of debt. Essentially, they were forced to work for free into perpetuity.

If Black farmers dared to protest or question their payment, the plantation owners had them arrested. Once they were considered criminals, they were forced to work for the same plantation owner for free. Since trying to run away was also a crime, anyone who was caught trying to escape was also forced to work for free. They had to work from sunup to sundown. Black sharecroppers faced the same punishments as they did during slavery and were subjected to public floggings or whippings simply for disagreeing.

If a plantation owner thought someone was planning a rebellion, they met it with violence. But now that they were no longer considered a white person's property, entire Black families faced threats of being lynched daily. Countless Black men, women, and children were lynched in 1865 alone. In response, Republicans tried to use white Southerner's terrorism to help themselves politically. Their aim was to get Black people the right to vote so they could use them to stay in office.

Not even a year after the war, Confederate officials were already in the new government.

Confederate politicians like Mayor John Monroe, Attorney General Andrew Herald, and Lt. Governor Albert Voorhies planned to help the South rise again. They deputized and armed hundreds of average white citizens to control the Black population.

In New Orleans, Black residents planned a convention to discuss how to deal with the Black Codes. When nearly 130 Black people marched toward the convention center holding the American flag, they were confronted by an armed mob, including deputized whites acting as police officers and firefighters. Once the group of Black residents crossed over Canal St., the mob became increasingly violent and threw bricks and bottles at them. After shots were fired, it quickly turned into a massacre.

The group shot up the convention center, then set it on fire with people still inside. Black men, women, and children tried to get away, but they were attacked and shot at from behind.

Some people tried to jump out of windows to get out of the building and away from the shooting. White women even cut and stabbed people to death. They attacked every Black person they came across. Many Black residents were pulled off streetcars and beaten in the middle of the street before being shot.

The official report said 50 people were killed and over 200 more were wounded. Other reports say over 200 Black people were killed and another 86 were wounded during the massacre. The actual number of deaths is unknown, but eventually, martial law was declared. Not one white citizen was arrested or indicted for the attack.

Now that chattel slavery was officially over, it became open season on Black men, women, and children. Not only were whites upset they lost free labor, they feared they'd have to compete for jobs. Many Black people thought the 13th Amendment brought an end to their nightmare, only for them to be facing a different form of terrorism. The New Orleans Massacre of 1866 was one of the first attacks, but it certainly wouldn't be the last.

EPILOGUE.

Although slavery isn't the beginning of our story, it certainly was a major turning point. The concept of race itself had already existed but Europeans were the first to use it as a measure of one's humanity. However, the system of white supremacy wasn't created overnight, it took centuries to cultivate. They had to strip us of our language, culture, religion, land, family, and every concept of self-identity. To maintain their system, it was important to eliminate any ideas of self-autonomy, self-respect, and most importantly, any ideas of freedom.

I got tired of us not knowing our history. It's so important for us to learn ourselves and our story that think tanks are created to ensure we never do. It became my mission to investigate anti-Black talking points and find out the truth.

So, I went back to the beginning of what became the Transatlantic Slave Trade and literally went year by year documenting our story from a Black perspective. Still, so much of our history was lost. It's important to learn our history no matter your age and it's never too late. However, my intention for writing this was to compile our documented history into book form and help the next generation continue to make progress in our advancement.

In future works, we'll continue this journey. But just as they worked to create this system, we must work twice as hard to overcome and eliminate it. And just as they maintained this practice over centuries, it may take generations to heal. We may never get back some things that were lost but it's important to relearn our worth and remember our value. Never let anyone else control your history because those who control your story can also control you. At the end of the day, we are all we got. We have to start standing for something or we'll keep falling for anything.

ACKNOWLEDGMENTS

I would like to acknowledge everyone who helped make this book possible. Thank you to my family for the support and understanding, not only during this process but throughout my journey of becoming woke. Thank you to my friends for the encouragement and advice to help me stay focused during tough times. A special thanks to my friend Tatiana who was the first to suggest transforming my work into a book series. I'd also like to thank all the extraordinarily intelligent people I've met on my path. You all have taught me so much. It's too many to name individually but I appreciate you all.

I would like to acknowledge my editor Jessica Berry. Thank you for being so kind and patient. You can reach her at jberryeditorial.com. I'd also like to thank my book formatter Arilia at Winn Publications. You can reach her at winnpublications.com. I must acknowledge a young talented graphic designer Danielle Page. You can reach her at daniellecpage.com. Thank you all so much.

Finally, I'd like to acknowledge the ancestors. Those who were mentioned in the book as well as those who weren't. Thank you to all those who gave their lives for us to be in a better position. Thank you to those who gave their blood, sweat, and tears. All the men and women who sacrificed time with their families in pursuit of the greater good. I can not thank you enough for protecting and preserving everything we have left. I'd also like to acknowledge those who are still here working towards progress. Thank you for the courage, strength, and inspiration to carry on.